Advance Praise

"Having experienced sexual harassment as a woman in more than one job I was left feeling hopeless, ashamed and wondering if I was doing something to attract this unwanted attention. I felt powerless against the people in positions of power perpetrating the harassment and would either ignore it hoping it would go away or I would quit. Every night I would weigh the toll it was taking on my mental health against the cost of feeding my child and financially supporting our home. Ignoring the behavior just led to escalation and quitting the job did not alleviate the stress only added to it as now I was starting at square one with a new company. I wish I had read "Career Defense 101" in my early 20's. Meredith Holley gives an easy to understand, intuitive and smart defense strategy to protect your career, integrity and mental health. She provides tangible examples, writing exercises and worksheets that put you in the driver seat rather than a passenger. You will walk away with a better grasp of the law and how it pertains to your situation, how to construct a support network, confronting your harasser (or not) and an action plan you can feel empowered by. A must read for all!"

~**JENNIFER TINSLEY**, Administrative Assistant,
Lane County Government

"There are plenty of books about sexual harassment and the legal claims involved. What Meredith Holley adds to that literature is an empowering roadmap to creating a life of success and meaning no matter what kind of harassment you are experiencing. All too often the true cost of sexual harassment is that women give up on themselves and their careers. This book covers the legal angles but more importantly it teaches women how to empower themselves to deal with harassment and to create thriving lives and careers not in spite of it, but because of it. A must-read for anyone experiencing harassment at work or anywhere else."

~**KARA LOEWENTHEIL**, J.D., M.C.C., host of the UnF*ck Your Brain Podcast and creator of UnF*ck Your Brain: A Feminist Blueprint for Creating Confidence, New York, NY

"The stories of real life women, the situations they experience, and how Meredith helped them will help you understand you are not alone if you experience harassment or assault in the workplace and - perhaps most importantly - that there are resources available to you. The book aides in demystifying how the law can be used in harassment/assault situations. Lawsuits, cease and desist - just the word the "law" in general - can feel overwhelming and daunting but Meredith breaks down the pros and cons of legal action in layman's terms. Even if you haven't experienced harassment in the workplace, this is a valuable read for anyone in the workplace. It can guide your supporters and allies - and even your adversaries - in understanding your approach when defending your career from a blow like harassment or assault."

~**KIRA O'CONNOR**, J.D., Public Policy Programs, EMEA, Instagram London, United Kingdom

"Meredith's stories are relatable, the strategies are tough assignments and the work is certain to be a game changer for those who wish to beat the odds and improve their lives."

~**JUDY**, Secondary Survivor

"EVERYONE should read Meredith Holley's Career Defense 101: the person experiencing harassment in their place of work, someone who wants to expand their knowledge of what others go through, and those that want to be allies for friends and colleagues going through this difficult thing in their life. Everyone has something to learn from this book. When reading, it feels like you are sitting down with an old friend for coffee and coming up with a plan for your life. She brings a difficult topic down to a level that is encouraging and practical. She lets you know it isn't always easy addressing sexual harassment in your own life, but it is possible, and things can be better."

~**LUCY DURST**, Deputy District Attorney
Jackson County Oregon

"What sets Meredith Holley's work apart from other self-help books for women facing harassment in the workplace is that it provides a truly valuable set of tools to empower women to take remedial action. Ms. Holley demystifies the law, giving candid and thoughtful advice about the obstacles posed by a patriarchal legal system that favors male harassers over women. She teaches with both compassion and humor, using real world examples and powerful analogies. This uplifting book is a must-read not just for women who struggle with sexual harassment, but for anyone entering the workplace and searching for fulfillment in their careers."

~**LESLIE O'LEARY**, Attorney
Eugene, Oregon

Career Defense 101

CAREER
defense 101

HOW TO STOP SEXUAL HARASSMENT
WITHOUT QUITTING YOUR JOB

MEREDITH HOLLEY

NEW YORK
LONDON • NASHVILLE • MELBOURNE • VANCOUVER

Career Defense 101

How to Stop Sexual Harassment Without Quitting Your Job

Published in New York, New York, by Morgan James Publishing in partnership with Difference Press. Morgan James is a trademark of Morgan James, LLC. www.MorganJamesPublishing.com

No part of this book is intended as legal advice. This book does not create an attorney-client relationship between you and the author. If you would like to get advice about how the law applies to your particular situation, please consult an attorney.

The names in this book have been changed to protect identities. The stories included really happened, but are written in a way to protect identities, such as combining some stories. If you asked the harassers involved their side, they would remember the stories differently.

ISBN 9781642791518 paperback
ISBN 9781642791532 case laminate
ISBN 9781642791525 eBook
Library of Congress Control Number: 2018907441

Cover and Interior Design by:
Chris Treccani
www.3dogcreative.net

Morgan James is a proud partner of Habitat for Humanity Peninsula and Greater Williamsburg. Partners in building since 2006.

Get involved today! Visit
MorganJamesPublishing.com/giving-back

For our mothers who spoke out and those who stayed quiet. For our daughters: may they have the courage to speak and be surrounded by those who listen.

"The moment we begin to fear the opinions of others and hesitate to tell the truth that is in us, and from motives of policy are silent when we should speak, the divine floods of light and life no longer flow into our souls. Every truth we see is ours to give the world, not to keep for ourselves alone, for in so doing we cheat humanity out of their rights and check our own development."

~ELIZABETH CADY STANTON

Table of Contents

Foreword

I almost dropped out of the case the day before the deadline. What changed everything for me, in making one of the biggest decisions of my life, was a conversation with one of my teammates. She said, "Chrissy, please do what is best for you, but can I ask what your biggest reservation is to not wanting to move forward?" I realized that the reason was I felt like I was being disloyal. I had to ask myself, "Disloyal to whom?" I had been trained to follow the leader, no matter whether they were taking me to heaven or to hell. We were trained not to question, but to listen and obey. But, I realized, if I went forward in joining this case, it was holding people accountable who had been disloyal to me, and, no matter how painful this realization was, that was more important. I did not owe them loyalty. I owed loyalty to the little girls who could be hurt later if I didn't tell my story. That was a turning point in identifying myself as a Sister Survivor, joining other sisters who helped shut down Dr. Larry Nassar.

I understand how it feels to not want to think about a topic like sexual harassment or abuse. But, if you are reading this book because you just want to be better informed, or whether you are dealing with your own experience, you are not alone. If you have experienced a trauma, you are not the first one. Currently, I am a stuntwoman, yoga instructor, former gymnast, wife, and mother of two children. I have a degree in psychology from Michigan State University. I started my entertainment career in *Tarzan Rocks!* at Disney World, but you may have seen me as a stuntwoman in *Iron Man, X-Men: First Class, Inception, The Dark Knight Rises, Terminator: Salvation, Star Trek, Spider-Man 3* and television shows like *Wonder Woman, CSI: NY, ER, American Horror Story,* and *Bones.* I have always been an athlete and love to compete. But, I did not just naturally understand how to protect myself from abuse, and it was not easy for me to start talking about my experience at Michigan State University. If you are experiencing something like that, I want you to know you're not alone.

It was tools like the tools in this book that made it possible for me to start protecting myself and become an advocate for the girls who will come after us and are vulnerable to abuse.

I went to Michigan State University through a full gymnastics scholarship. On most teams in my experience, as an athlete, when you are injured, you become invisible because you can't contribute. I was so injured at one point that I was barely making it. Dr. Larry Nassar treated our gymnastics team, and treatment was mandatory. As gymnasts, we were trained that whether we were comfortable or not, we had to obey the adults around us. Treatment was required in the handbook, and we could jeopardize losing our scholarships and our place on the team if we refused to accept treatment. But, it was more complicated than that because as an injured athlete, Dr. Nassar was often the only person who acted nice. He would give us drills, and pay attention to us, and it seemed like he was the only person who cared. Part of the "treatment" he gave us was actually sexual abuse, which many of us did not realize at the time because we were so trained to obey.

I now know that this is typical "grooming" behavior that sexual predators use to create loyalty with their victims, but at the time I had never heard the word "grooming." It was shocking when we found out how many adults knew gymnasts were being sexually abused, including law enforcement as far up as the FBI. A lot of us are still sorting through what happened because it doesn't seem real.

When I started as a stuntwoman and was learning how to fight, I had a lot of fear that using my own power and being forceful was wrong. I would apologize if I would accidentally make contact with someone during a fight scene, which definitely didn't look right on camera. I had to learn how to use my power both in my stunt work, and when people crossed a line with me in real life. Although this process initially was difficult, the more I practiced the more empowered I became.

Around 2010, I found the life coaching tools that Meredith includes in this book. At the time, I did not have the language to call my experience at the Michigan State University sexual abuse. I just thought I had a lot of mental issues, but soon realized I had to work through my destructive behaviors because I was quickly allowing them to take over my life. Coaching helped save me. I learned to look at my experience from a "watcher" perspective, which helped me understand I had a choice in how to move forward, even if I didn't see one right away.

It was tough to learn how to find my voice and use it to protect myself and advocate for other people, but it has saved my life. Once, I was confronted on the street by someone prepared to attack me, and because I responded unapologetically, the man backed down right away. I realized this is what is possible when you find your power. I don't walk around always unafraid, but if someone crosses a line with me, I have learned how to use anything that is necessary to protect myself.

When I first agreed to join other gymnasts as a Sister Survivor and go forward with supporting the criminal and civil cases around the abuse at Michigan State University, I was still processing a lot of it. Doing my own healing and learning how to protect myself was different than using my experience for advocacy. I decided to go forward as a Jane Doe at first, rather than using my real name, because I was truly ashamed and embarrassed. I also had to consider my husband and children, and I did not want my name to be associated with the name of someone who abused me.

Ultimately, I decided to use my name in the legal process and in other advocacy because of the children I know are still vulnerable to being abused. In the summer of 2018, I attended a Congressional hearing with my other Sister Survivors. One little girl, who was only 10 years old, was there, and as she told the legislators her name, she cried. I don't know any adult who can say they're okay with seeing a child go through what this little girl has been through. I realized it is our responsibility as adults to keep this conversation going and make change.

At the beginning, it felt easier for me to come forward only as a Jane Doe because of how deeply ashamed and embarrassed I was. It may be easier for you to walk away from this book and pretend things are okay in your workplace (even if it's not). But, there are little girls who will be affected by harassment and abuse if we walk away. If you are experiencing harassment or abuse, you deserve something better, and creating that is possible.

It took me a long time to come to the conclusion that I am a Sister Survivor. I resisted it because I thought it might mean I was a victim, that my voice didn't matter, or that standing up to abuse would make me have to face that the people I trusted the most around me didn't protect me or my teammates. Now I know that it means I am an adult who is willing to protect little girls coming after me. It is uncomfortable to share my story publicly, but it is worth it.

You are worthy of a better experience, and that starts with getting information like the information in this book. Whatever is going on with you, there are sisters who have come before you. They were scared too. But they realized that if they didn't take action, the abuse would likely continue.

I found out about *Career Defense 101* through a mutual friend, when I spoke at the National Women's Law Center Gala in 2018. After looking more into Meredith's work and the book, what stands out to me is that Meredith is not only a lawyer, but is also someone who has experienced harassment herself, and so she understands how powerless it can feel. In this book she teaches how to navigate the law and use it in your favor, and also how to manage your thinking and set effective boundaries so that you can find *your* voice. Meredith recognizes that trauma exists and can interfere with our abilities to fully live our lives, but also that there are solutions and that trauma is not a death sentence.

We can all learn how to process our trauma and how to communicate in difficult, emotional situations, and *Career Defense 101* is contributing methods and strategies for doing that.

If there is one thing I would hope you get from this book and this letter to you, it is that your voice matters! I believed for a long time that it did not matter whether I said anything about the abuse I experienced. I was trained to believe that my opinion didn't matter, and that I just needed to do what superiors told me to do. As a child, my life would have been a living hell if I argued with that, but as an adult I have the opportunity to change it. A lot of people don't realize they have choices in how to respond to harassment and abuse. Choices are always there. We can all learn to communicate better, and it's through finding our voices that we will do that.

Your voice is important!

Chrissy Weathersby Ball
Sister Survivor, Stuntwoman, Certified Life Coach & Yoga Instructor
Dallas, Texas

Introduction

Stunned

When we first experience something offensive that starts to interfere with our careers, it is often hard for us to even wrap our brains around what is happening. When Anna came to me to see if she had a legal claim, she was working on a high-level business deal with a much older man who started harassing her. He invited her to stay in his home while she was visiting for business, and he soon began touching and propositioning her. When she was writing a description of what happened to her, she repeated over and over, "I was stunned." I asked her to be more specific about whether she was afraid or just surprised, and she kept saying, "I was just stunned! I was shocked. I couldn't believe it was happening."

I recognized in Anna what happens to almost all of the clients who come to me, as a trial lawyer and coach, with sexual harassment claims, and what happened to me early in my career. When we encounter harassment, our brains just do not compute what is happening. Is this really happening? Is this okay? Could this be legal? We are often so shocked that we can't even respond in the moment. Sometimes, we don't want to know the answer. We just want to ignore it until it goes away.

Unfortunately, ignoring and avoiding inappropriate, harassing behavior does not make it go away.

Ignoring It

One of the first clients I worked with on a sexual harassment claim, as both a trial lawyer and coach, was Naomi. She had worked her way up from an accounts receivable position in a lumber yard to a position running the yard's indoor store (though she didn't actually get the pay or title she deserved for her work). In the meantime, as she was working her way up, the general manager was sexually harassing her. He was making comments about her appearance, propositioning her, having explosive tantrums, going through her cell phone, and even trying to take pictures of her in the bathroom.

Naomi had decided to ignore the harassment and try to focus on her work. After all, the general manager would say he was joking about a lot of the comments, or he would apologize later, and she was tough. She was not a victim. She knew his comments were disrespectful and even threatening, not hilarious jokes, but she did not want to make a big deal out of something it seemed like she should be able to brush off. She loved her job and loved the authority she had in the store. Sometimes, customers, too, were inappropriate with her, but with them, she knew she had the power to make them leave, and they needed her expertise. She could shut that harassment down without carrying it home and worrying about it at night. The customers did not phase her, but when she was alone with the manager, she felt constant anxiety.

Naomi felt her only option was to ignore the behavior and hope it would go away. She thought that if she did anything about it, even if she told anyone, it would become a huge situation and she would lose her job and her reputation. She believed that people would say it was not a big deal, and she should just toughen up. Or, she thought, they would think it was a big deal and she was lying about it. She and her partner were supporting a family, and she could not afford to lose her job or her reputation. She felt embarrassed, and, in the back of her mind, she wondered if she was doing something to cause the harassment.

At first, even though she knew most of this man's behavior was inappropriate, she did not identify it as harassment. Then, she invited a friend, Diana, to work with her, knowing it would be a great job opportunity for Diana, who was a single mom. When Naomi saw the manager doing the same things to her friend, suddenly it was different. She knew, watching the manager go through Diana's cell phone pictures, snap her bra, and lift up her skirt, that none of it was okay. She knew that Diana had done nothing to deserve this treatment, and then her own situation became clearer as well.

But, Naomi still felt trapped and did not know what to do. If there was nothing Naomi and Diana were doing to cause the harassment, was there anything they could do to make it stop? Diana quit the job, even though it was a huge blow to herself and her little daughter. She knew she could not raise her daughter to expect respectful behavior from men if she did not model that strength. Diana was willing to lose thousands of dollars to protect her daughter and avoid sexual harassment.

Naomi stayed. She did not feel like she had other options, and she had invested eight years in this position. She wanted to continue to advance in the company where she had invested so much time and money.

She came to me, wanting to find out if she could file a lawsuit for equal pay because she was paid less than her male colleagues. Mostly, she just wanted to present a legal argument to her company to make them listen and increase her salary to a fair amount. Equal pay claims can be very difficult, but I looked through Naomi's meticulous documentation, and I was impressed. As we were talking, Naomi became more comfortable and started telling me about her general manager touching and propositioning her. She told me how she had gained weight, and now she was starting to lose her hair because of the stress. Eventually, in that conversation or one of the many others we had as she was processing her experience, Naomi told me how she had tried to ignore his threatening behavior, how she knew he had a gun at home, and she would worry about that sometimes.

She decided to go through the difficult, painful process of reporting the harassment and filing a legal claim. Naomi was still working, while we were deciding how to go forward, and she sometimes had to be alone in the store with the general manager. She started having panic attacks as she pulled into her work parking lot, and her doctor decided to restrict her from going to work because of her increasing anxiety. During the course of the case, she became more and more anxious, depressed, and even agoraphobic. She was proud of herself for standing up to the harassment, but it took a huge toll on her health and wellbeing. Her partner was worried about her, and she had very little tolerance for their children's difficult behavior.

At the time, I did not have the strategies I use now with my clients, and watching Naomi's process motivated me to find something better. It was not enough for me, although it was important, that I have the skills to advocate for my clients through the legal system. I wanted more for them. I wanted Naomi and the other women I was working with to see what superheroes they were and to get all of the success and respect I knew they deserved. I wanted them to walk proudly, free from harassment, and create the life of their dreams.

Resilience

While the law has done a lot to help women have more access to traditionally male roles, I am never shocked when a woman does not want to bring a legal claim for harassment. While I was working as a trial lawyer for a law firm, I always told clients, "It is better to have a good job than a good legal claim." What I meant was that if my clients can successfully defend their careers from sexual harassment, they will probably save hundreds of thousands of dollars, not just in legal expenses, but in actual pay. Plus, lawsuits, while completely worthwhile and one of the last ways we have to create justice and safety in our communities, are very stressful and painful. Wanting a lawsuit would be like saying, "I hope I can see someone drowning in the ocean and have the opportunity to jump in and save them." People who are willing to bring lawsuits do so to protect all of us from injustice and keep our communities safe, but the process itself is emotionally and physically difficult. Anything financial they get from a lawsuit almost never makes up for what they have experienced, but knowing they can make the community safer moves them forward.

In part, this is also because the law can only step in when something has gone really wrong – when someone has been physically injured, fired, or forced to quit because of harassment. The law only addresses a very narrow set of circumstances, and often when women look for legal help, like with Naomi, the law can only offer one part of the solution they need. Her legal claim could hold her company accountable for creating a harassing environment, but it, in itself, could not get her a good job or even teach her the mental resilience she needed to survive the legal claim.

I have often seen other trial lawyers talk about whether a client is "able to follow through with a claim," and what they mean is that they are not sure that a client has the mental resilience to be able to tell her story over and over. Rather than develop skills to teach this resilience to clients, trial lawyers often assume that someone either has it or she doesn't. They assume that people who don't present with it right away won't be able to be successful in a legal claim. This is unfortunate because often the people who do not show mental resilience right away are the tough people, like Naomi, who spent years trying to ignore trauma. That very skill of ignoring trauma is often the challenge, and even the undoing, of women who want to speak out about harassment.

We were able to successfully resolve Naomi's equal-pay and sexual-harassment claims (and the claims for Diana, who supported Naomi throughout this experience), but by that time, Naomi was afraid to leave her house and was mired in depression and anxiety. While the resolution of the claims was a big win, and those of us on the outside could see how it acknowledged everything Naomi had been though, it did not bring Naomi back into control of her life. She felt unhealthy and afraid most of the time.

After I put together the career defense strategies that I teach in this book and in trainings, I went back to Naomi and asked her to try a pilot program, using them. By the end of the program, she was starting a job she loved and had a completely new outlook on her future. It was incredible to see the transformation she was able to make in six short weeks.

I have seen client after client try to ignore and avoid sexual harassment, either until the time limits for bringing a lawsuit have passed or until they have built up so much trauma that, like Naomi, it takes a toll on their physical and mental wellbeing. I see women quit jobs, move laterally, or decide not to go for promotions in order to avoid men harassing them, and – even though I completely understand why and I would never blame anyone for doing that – this is costing women and their families way too much time and money. Then, many women go to a lawyer, looking for help, and all they get is a legal claim (if they are lucky and even have a legal claim). I do believe in the civil justice system, and I think jury trials are important in order to keep our communities safe when something has gone really wrong. But, when women are losing time and money in their careers because of sexual harassment, lawsuits are not enough.

In this book, I focus on my work with clients who identify as women, though I have worked with clients who identify as men or as nonbinary, and people from many races and economic backgrounds. I focus on women in order to be upfront about my own experience, privileges, and challenges. I am a white woman, and the majority of people I have worked with in these claims are white women, so that is the particular area of my experience and expertise. I also focus on men as the perpetrators of harassment because, while I have seen instances of women harassing both women and men, the majority of my experience is with men as the harassers, and that is statistically more common as well.

My focus in this book is meant to be upfront about both the expertise and limits of my experience, not to exclude anyone. I have seen the strategies in this book applied successfully with all genders and races, and each situation is unique and deserves unique attention and strategic planning. The career defense strategies in this book are strategies that I have seen be successful with client after client in defending their careers from sexual harassment so that they can advance in fulfilling work.

Sometimes, it is not enough to know that strategies will work for us. We know we are strong enough to deal with anything life throws at us, and it sounds, frankly, terrifying to confront sexism in the people we love and work with. But, in the back of our minds we know that if we don't deal with the sexism we are facing, it could hurt someone else. Like Naomi, it is easier for us to help Diana than to help ourselves. We see little girls around us and want so much better for them, but it is hard to think about expecting and demanding something better for ourselves.

I developed these strategies for myself because if I know that if I thrive in my career, I can help you thrive in yours. I developed these strategies for you because I know if you thrive in your career, that helps me thrive in mine. I developed these strategies for all of the people whose lives I know you are meant to influence, and all of the little girls who will be inspired by your courage, but who may not be able to hear your voice yet because it has been muffled by sexism. Even if it is hard to value the importance of implementing these strategies for yourself and your own success, please consider how important it is for the rest of us to see you shine.

Chapter 1

——— ✳ ———

Strong Women, Troubled Men

"I never thought of myself as a battered wife.
I was a very strong woman in love with a deeply troubled man."
— LESLIE MORGAN STEINER,
TED: "Why domestic violence victims don't leave."

When Naomi first came to my office and described her experiences trying to ignore and manage the constant harassment at work, I understood. I had similar experiences of my own to pull from. But, even though I had not fully compiled the strategies in this book, I knew that it was possible to use those experiences to build strength. Leslie Morgan Steiner, in her brilliant TED Talk, "Why domestic violence victims don't leave," explains that when she was with her abusive husband, "I never thought of myself as a battered wife. I was a very strong woman in love with a deeply troubled man."

When I say that I have seen harassment build strength, I do not mean that the strength comes from managing men's troubled behavior. Naomi knew that trying to use her strength to manage her colleague's harassment was killing her. She was literally losing hair and having panic attacks when she pulled into the parking lot at work. She was ready to learn a different strength.

Discrimination Detector

I am sometimes reluctant to tell clients about my background because when any of us compare our experiences, we jump right into saying, "I'm not experiencing real sexism." No matter who had the more extreme experience, we either feel like the bigger victim or the bigger whiner. So, I share this because I have had the great privilege of seeing life through the lens of straightforward, honest sexism, but not to compare any of our experiences.

When you grow up with the lessons I learned as a kid, you can see the outgrowths of sexism clearly, without the shame people have if they were raised to believe "sexism is evil." I've noticed that when people believe that sexism is evil, it contributes to their need to ignore and avoid it, which does not help end it. I would not have identified it as "sexism" when I was young because I was raised to understand it was "the truth."

I have one of those backgrounds that seems normal to me, but that I know has some shock value when I announce it in public. "I was raised in a cult." My brother likes to test out different ways to tell people to create the best shock value, but I'm so demure that I would never. Other than writing it in a book.

I was raised in a religious cult, and its core message was that women are evil. I went through a phase in my life where I thought that maybe I was exaggerating when I said that, but my brother, who is an investigative journalist, revisited the cult as an adult and assures me that I am not exaggerating.

I remember, as a 7-year-old, reading one of the magazines that the cult published and seeing a cartoon. The cartoon showed a young heterosexual couple, with a barrel chested, huge man, and a tiny child-like woman. I believe they were in wedding clothes. It had six frames, and in each frame, the woman got bigger as the man got smaller, until the woman was obese, and the man was in a casket.

The cartoon and the message of the cult had a big impact on me as a little girl. I knew there was something wrong with my mom (a message that she whole-heartedly believed), and that my dad was the head of the household. I knew that if I got bigger, it would hurt men.

(I have never been able to find this cartoon again, so if you find it, send it to me at Meredith@FreedomResourceCenter.com. Important note: I do not, however, recommend googling "cartoon woman gets bigger man gets smaller." Awkward results. Don't say I didn't warn you.)

Our family did not stay in the religious cult, and although my parents loudly proclaimed the evils of hypnotism and indoctrination, their core values did not change – women were still evil. They shifted to attending mainstream mega churches, but it was not very different to hear about why women should remain silent in church and can't become pastors than to openly hear explanations about why women are evil. At that point, I believed that message, and so the contemporary Christian dressing up of "women are evil" didn't even seem like lipstick on a pig. It was like lipstick on your friend who your parents bring to Thanksgiving every year. In my understanding, it was just the truth.

I became a feminist in college, which was the first time I read that feminism was not about destroying men, but about helping women. I was shocked. I went home and showed what I had read to my roommate. She, having grown up in the same small town as I, was also shocked. We had long conversations, even losing sleep, about the possibility that feminism was about helping women, not destroying men. (I'm not going to lie, I think that within the past six months we have had a conversation, losing sleep, about how feminism is not about men. Some conversations are just worth having over and over.) We imagined what that could look like for us. We wanted to help women, but we had never wanted to be shrill.

Don't worry, we eventually became the shrill feminists we were always meant to be.

Strong and Brave

Because I had such clear, shameless messages as a child that women are evil, and that women deserve less than men, I have always recognized those messages more clearly than many people around me. I believed this as an innocent child and deliberately decided to change the belief as a young adult. So, I can see where it comes through in culture – sometimes on a muted level and sometimes as directly as I experienced it when I was little.

This is the invisible gorilla test that Daniel Kahneman talks about in *Thinking Fast and Slow*. In the invisible gorilla experiment, researchers asked participants to count how many times people in a video passed a basketball back and forth. While the players passed the basketball, a person in a gorilla suit walked through the group. The study showed that when participants were focused on the players passing the ball, they did not even notice the person in the gorilla suit. Once researchers pointed out the gorilla, though, it was impossible to miss. This shows that selective attention narrows our ability to perceive the whole picture.

But, when we know a person in a gorilla suit might walk by (or when we know that the idea that women are evil is possible and acceptable to a lot of people), we can recognize it.

After college, and embracing the idea of being a feminist, I moved to Ukraine as a Peace Corps volunteer because I wanted to prove myself through helping. Ukraine in the early 2000s was another place where the message that women deserved less than men was openly embraced. I was teaching a 9th grade class on Valentine's Day, and I decided to do an exercise that forced them to use the descriptive words they were learning. I said they needed to write a love story between a man and a woman (I know, heteronormative, but I was making baby steps with them), and first they needed to describe both characters.

The woman was strong and brave, they said. She worked hard and had big muscles.

The man was very beautiful and kind, they told me. He was good at cooking and had stylish clothes.

At first, I was so excited. All of my lessons about gender stereotypes were paying off! Then, I realized what was happening. I realized before the students did, and I got them to pretty thoroughly describe the story before they started yelling.

"No, Ms. Holley!" they said. "We moved the words! We have the wrong words!" I innocently told them I had no idea what they were talking about. "The woman is not strong and brave!" they said. "And the man is not beautiful and kind!!" They were jumping out of their seats to fix the error, which was pretty outrageous for a Ukrainian classroom, where the students were taught that their elbows could never leave their desks. I was laughing hysterically at them.

"I'm strong and brave. Right?" I asked. "I moved to a different country just to meet all of you." They conceded the point, but they were incredibly disturbed about the mistake. We had another lesson on gender stereotypes, which was one of my favorite experiences of my time in Ukraine. The students were brilliant, and, like me as a child, they had no shame around sharing the sexism they were raised with.

While I was in Ukraine, I also had the chance to create a program that allowed my high school students to tutor elementary school students from the local orphanage (all participants ended up, not by design, being girls). It was so fun to be able to openly work to challenge what girls were capable of, with kids whose lessons on gender were so similar to what mine had been growing up. I saw in these girls the assumption that they were allowed to be smart, as long as they used it in a nurturing way – as with volunteering to tutor – but, they would not speak out and would defer to boys they knew were wrong in class.

At the same time that I was doing all of this good work, however, I was being stalked by a music teacher who had been fired from the music institute for molesting his female students. He would call my home and talk with my host mother. He would show up at my school. Early on, my host teacher told me it would be a good idea to go to a private violin concert with this stalker. We went to the Palace of Culture, which was a local performance theater, and he played the violin, to a giant theater with an audience of only me and my host teacher, with the accompaniment of a boom box playing R&B.

The Peace Corps had trouble responding to the issue, and, at some point, one of the security directors resigned – I believe at least in part because of the conflict around how to appropriately respond. Ultimately, security decided that I could be safe in the town, despite this music teacher's phone calls and constant presence, as long as I let my students know that I would need to leave the town if I saw him again. I found out in my exit interview that he had come to the school multiple times, and the school had just withheld that information from me. But, at the same time, I knew that my students and their families cared about me and would keep me safe. I knew I had advocates in the nursing staff at Peace Corps. I knew each of the volunteers in my cohort was family and would do anything for me. I had resources.

When I was leaving, my 9th grade class (I'm one to pick favorites, and they were far and away my favorites) asked me why I went to Ukraine. I told them, "I wanted to help you." They looked confused.

"We don't need your help," they said.

I laughed. "I know that now," I said, "Thank you for helping me."

That experience gave me a tremendous amount of dissonance around my idea that I would help the disadvantaged in contrast to my own sense of being vulnerable and unsafe. For much of my experience,

I was being stalked and I couldn't buy food without help. How would I help the people I wanted to help? What could I offer if I was in danger myself?

I learned in Ukraine that often I was safe, when it seemed like I might be in danger. I also learned that my discomfort and unhappiness did not, in itself, help anybody. Just because something seemed hard or dangerous to me did not mean I was helping someone else. I had to re-evaluate what I wanted from life and how I could contribute to others through my own happiness and fulfillment.

Strategy

Embracing the identity of "shrill feminist," which we often have to do to talk about sexist messages in culture, might be courageous, but it does not create a sense of belonging or ease. Even if we insider feminists know that it is okay to be shrill if it means standing up for other women, it assumes that we are outsiders to the other people we love. We are still the witches walking the line between advocacy and death by fire. It is so worth it, but it is not something we wish on our daughters.

Driving down the street at 26 years old, I remember thinking, "I wonder if it is possible for me to go to law school?" I wondered if I would be smart enough or if it was true that women really were more inclined to be good at, like, baking cookies than thinking. I offer that, not because I think there is any legitimacy to the idea that women belong in the kitchen, but to say that I was a college educated, former Peace Corps volunteer, who was about to rise to the top of her class in law school, and I got there just by being curious about whether I was even smart enough to be accepted to law school.

My thinking and my experience were incredibly dissonant. I had been trained to believe that women were somehow inferior at our core, and my feminist beliefs were so contrary to that. My brain reconciled this by resolving on the idea that while my women friends were naturally amazing at everything they did, especially legal advocacy, I needed to work really hard to prove I belonged. I so overshot this hard work that in aiming for the middle of the class, I became one of the top four students in my first-year class and received an extra scholarship. I was shocked.

I waited for the day when people would find out that I did not really belong in the law.

And don't worry, it came!

Early in my legal career, I interviewed for an advocacy position. In one of the interviews, I was at lunch with an older male executive in the company, when suddenly it seemed like I was on a date. I couldn't tell you what happened to change the atmosphere, but it was palpable. I remember the exact moment it happened, and the way the executive changed his posture and leaned forward slightly, as I leaned back. I went to a group interview later that week, and the same executive escorted me around, gentlemanly, with his hand on my low back. I was very uncomfortable. He told me that they were not hiring, but if they found someone "particularly attractive" they might consider opening a position.

I got the position.

My supervisor was a woman, and, before I started, I decided to ask her advice about how to set good boundaries with the creepy executive. I told her nothing had become inappropriate, but I thought it might become inappropriate, so I wanted to make sure it was clear that I was at work to do my job and to be recognized for my work.

My supervisor said, "I'm really surprised to hear that because the last person in this position worked really closely with him, she never said anything, and she's really pretty."

This devolved into a mortifying conversation about whether I am pretty. The other piece of advice she gave me was that our work is just really sexist and we have to deal with it. She did not have the skills or tools to teach me what I needed, and, like many women, she had done what she could to survive and be successful without them.

When I started work, the creepy executive quickly began to give me back rubs, rub my arms and shoulders, lean his entire body against me, criticize my clothing, and reprimand me for talking when (I found out later) he was dramatically pausing during stories. I had no idea what to do. I did not want to talk to my supervisor again because I did not want to have a conversation about whether I was pretty enough to be harassed. I wanted strategies that worked.

I decided that it was not really happening and I was just so nervous in this job and anxious about doing good work that I was over-reacting. I decided that I could change my clothes and maybe that would make the job easier. I gained 40 pounds.

I was a lawyer, I thought. I should know how to handle myself. What was wrong with me that I did not deserve his respect? Maybe I just didn't belong in the law.

I was constantly afraid. I felt fear throughout the day. I wanted to leave the job, but that would mean giving up my career. My mentors didn't know what was going on, but told me to stick out my job even though I was unhappy and things would get better. I started experiencing suicidal thoughts, which I thought I had overcome years before.

I knew I needed to make a change, and I did.

Through my legal research, the thought management work I was trained in, and learning through my own experiences, I developed a career defense training that I have tested and tried with myself and my clients. Using the strategies in my training, I was able to have a conciliatory conversation with the creepy executive, in which he apologized and committed to change. He followed through with that change, we worked together for years after, and I left on good terms with that organization. I defended my career, using careful, deliberate strategies.

As is typical in the law, I have been called an assistant (and I have been told that John, the real assistant, must actually be an associate), criticized for my speech pattern (I talked too collaboratively), clothes (I exposed my shoulders), and I have constantly said too much or too little. I heard from older women attorneys that this is just the way the law is. It's sexist, but, like Leslie Morgan Steiner said, we are strong women, working with very troubled men.

Even today, I was arguing with a judge about a rule change, and I was explaining to her that if that rule had been in place years ago, people would not have been able to speak out about the sex abuse perpetrated by the Boy Scouts and the Catholic Church. She said, "That argument is emotional, so it's not useful. We help people by procedures in the courts, and that's what will bring justice." She cared about my argument, herself, but she believed that the other people in the room (men) would not. I understand her argument. I understand where the older women, who have helped me so much and paved the way for me, come from in managing the troubled men around them.

But, it is time for us to overcome the thinking errors that allow harassment to continue.

Using the strategies in this book, I have seen clients defend their careers by ending harassment within their jobs or by leaving to go on to something better – rather than quitting before it is the best solution for them. In each instance, they have created change that empowers them and contributes to ending sexual harassment in our culture.

The strategies are not easy, but they work to make real change and to show you how powerful you really are.

Chapter 2

Talk

"You shouldn't tell that story to people. It makes you sound weak," a guy I knew in law school said. I had just told him how, when I lived in Ukraine, I visited my friend Vanessa in central Ukraine. We got on a bus alone, with only ourselves and the two bus drivers, late at night. We expected the bus drivers to take us back to her area of town. Instead, they drove out into the corn fields and tried to feel us up. They asked us if we liked to party, as Vanessa gathered keys and a broken antenna as weapons around her. We both looked out into the dark cornfields as the bus drove away from town, thinking we may have to fight these men or run out into the fields to save ourselves.

I spoke Russian, not Ukrainian, and so Vanessa yelled at the bus drivers for both of us. Ultimately, they looked at the weapons, looked at each other, and the driver at the steering wheel broke into a sweat. They understood that we were not going to make things easy for them, and they drove us back into Vanessa's town.

When I worked in trial court, just after law school, I realized that what happened to Vanessa and me in Ukraine was kidnapping. It had never occurred to me before.

I told the law school guy what I had realized, and he warned me that I would sound weak if I kept talking about that experience. I was so surprised! Do war veterans sound weak when they talk about escaping capture? Do super heroes look weak when they convince their enemies to drop their evil scheme? How could I sound weak because of a bus driver trying to feel me up? The only explanation I could come up with was that this guy believed I was kidnapped because of something I had done. He wanted to believe that he would have been too smart or strong to be kidnapped and that it only happened to me because of my weakness.

This makes sense, and cognitive bias research describes it as the fundamental attribution error and optimism bias. Basically, all of us think other people got where they are because of something about who they are, and we don't want to believe bad things happen to good people (or that might mean that bad things will happen to us). For example, attorneys representing women who were injured by misdiagnoses of breast cancer receive the advice not to have any women on their jury because women will subconsciously be afraid that misdiagnosis could happen to them and not want to believe it actually happened to the woman bringing the claim.

I tend to think the stories where I escaped danger or overcame harassment are my most interesting, and so I am not inclined to stop telling them, but my law school classmate's comment did give me some insight into why women so often talk in hushed tones and only to each other about their harassment and abuse experiences. Some people will misunderstand.

The trouble with following that thinking is that it makes sure nothing changes. In order to really change harassment and end harassment in our own life, we need to be able to talk about it.

Hygiene

As I'm writing this, there has been a tidal wave of conversation about sexual harassment in the news. Of course, this type of wave has happened before and is often followed by what Susan Faludi identified as a backlash of cultural push against the growth that talking about harassment represents. A harasser gets elected to the Presidential office, women march and hashtag #MeToo, and then other women write letters defending flirting in the workplace. Cultural growth comes because of this push back and forth, but it is easy to feel torn and caught in the tide.

When my friends talked to me, hesitantly, about posting #MeToo on Facebook, many of them were worried that their harassment experience was not "real" harassment. Others were worried that men at work would approach them to talk about their post, intending to support them, and bring back flashbacks of sexual assault. I truly believe that what we say about our own harassment experiences is our own business, and there is no obligation to talk about any personal experience.

I also believe that each time we tell our own story it makes the problem real for the people around us and gives them motivation to actually press for change. On November 9, 2016, I woke up understanding that a man who openly admitted to sexual harassment would be taking over power in the United States. I realized that people I knew and loved had voted for him or not taken the issue seriously enough to cast a vote. I realized that if people I knew and loved were willing to do that, I was not loud enough about what it meant to me personally. Your experience and your story are important to the people around you. It is your choice, of course, whether talking about it is healthy for you, but I know sharing our honest stories changes the people around us.

Here's my theory:

Discrimination is like snot. Every nose has snot, and every brain has discrimination. I like to picture what society was like when we first found out that germs kill people. I think that there were some early adopters in hand washing who totally got it. They cared about stopping disease, and it was worth it to them to wash their hands. Particularly brave early adapters may have even encouraged other people to wash their hands.

But, there have to have been people who thought they were smarter than science, right? There have to have been people who thought it was disrespectful to ask for hand washing. "Who does she think she is, telling me that my hands are dirty?" the traditionalist would think, "I washed them this year! I have two friends who wash their hands all the time! I'll teach her about hand washing. My nose doesn't even have snot." Then they would blow their noses into their hands and wipe them on her food.

Hopefully, you see where I'm going with this. Hand washing revolutionized medicine, but I am positive that not everyone was happy about it. There may have even been those who denied that their particular noses carried germs.

That's the place we're in related to discrimination right now. All brains have discrimination. Discrimination is simply misattributing abilities or qualities to a person based on unrelated characteristics. For example, "People with yellow shirts are good at basketball" is a good example of discrimination because yellow shirts don't create basketball skills, just like having certain reproductive organs doesn't make a person better or worse at a work skill. The fact that our brains make these misattributions is science, and misattributions are called cognitive bias. Cognitive biases break down into smaller categories related to discrimination like group attribution error, the halo effect, and in-group bias. Many people are not ready to make a routine of washing their thinking, though.

Pointing out someone's bias is like saying, "Hey, you have a booger in your nose." Some people would rather not know about their boogers and would rather pretend their noses don't have snot. Some people want to blame the patient who died from infection and call her weak, rather than calling the doctor out for failing to wash his hands before surgery. Sadly, along the same lines, some people would rather not acknowledge that their brains make misattributions.

In terms of sexism, the thinking error comes down to the simple thought, "Women and men deserve different benefits and burdens." This thinking glitch is simple, but it plays out in horrific ways in society – from seeing the best and brightest among us being relegated to service jobs, low pay, and crushed dreams to rampant violence.

Thinking Errors

I think the quote attributed to Margaret Atwood is my favorite description of what I see as typical gender-based biases: "Men are afraid women will laugh at them. Women are afraid men will kill them."

This is the core of what we can do to create hygiene routines around gender discrimination. From a woman's perspective, the quickest thing our brains go to is to try to solve this by thinking, "Men need to stop killing us and being so sensitive." I don't have a man's perspective, but I imagine it to be something like, "Other men need to stop killing women, and women should respect me for being an ally."

That is such disempowering thinking on both sides. Both women and men in those examples are saying that ending discrimination is in someone else's hands – and someone they don't respect at that. But it is very typical thinking (noses have snot), and don't worry! If you have that thinking, I have good news. There is so much you can do to end discrimination just in your own mind, without all of the power to end discrimination being in the hands of murder-y men. Once you start working towards ending discrimination in your own mind, it is *so* much easier to help other people do the same.

The way you do it is by managing your own thinking. For women, it often seems really important to maintain the thinking that men could kill them. This turns up in every part of our lives, from the workplace to the grocery store parking lot, to home. Gavin de Becker is a threat assessment and violence expert. In his brilliant book, *The Gift of Fear*, he explains that women tend to have a more developed intuitive sense of actual danger than men do, but often we either do not listen to it or we dull that sense by seeing danger everywhere.

For example, Athena, a lawyer who consulted with me about harassment from a male colleague, told me that every time the colleague raised his voice with her, her heart started pounding and she froze like an animal encountering a predator. She also had flashbacks to her father, who had been physically abusive to her and her siblings as a child. All of this was going on in her head, while her colleague was yelling to someone else about a disorganized file. His yelling was clearly not a physical threat, but her body responded like it was. And nobody would blame her. Based on her experience, her brain was being incredibly smart to be sensitive to the threat.

Men are one of the leading causes of death to women, and so it makes sense that we are afraid.

But, at the same time, Athena was not actually in physical danger, and the helpful system her brain was using to protect her was not useful in that situation. Her brain thought she was being attacked by a giant bear, when really she was just witnessing a tantrum. Because her thinking shut her down, it was actually disempowering her instead of saving her.

I was talking about this thinking error with a male friend of mine, who is a particularly self-aware, thoughtful person. I told him the Margaret Atwood quote, and he said, "Oh, that is so spot on. Because for a man, being laughed at really is worse than death."

My friend missed the point of the quote, but, at the same time, I think he hit on an important piece of this that really does unite women and men. Men may have very little evidence (that I can work out, anyway) that a woman laughing will kill him, but perhaps men often have sensitive shame triggers where women have sensitive fear triggers.

As my friend explained, many men may quickly associate laughter with shame and rejection and think death preferable to a life of shame.

So, I am in one corner believing that a man yelling or touching my shoulder without permission means my death is imminent. My friend is in another corner, believing that a woman's laughter means something shameful about him that is worse than death. And both of us think the other's thinking error is preferable.

If we needed to stop men from being violent and stop women from laughing in order to end discrimination, we would be screwed. Luckily, managing our own thinking and being deliberate about identifying our thinking errors is much easier than trying to cover the world in padding.

The overarching rule for correcting a thinking error is this: *Talk about it!*

You don't have to talk about it in a vindictive or mean way, but just putting light on the problem is a huge step. Tell people about your thinking errors and be open to talk about it if you are curious whether you see one in someone else. (Tell your friends when they have boogers hanging out of their noses, and blow your own nose when appropriate!) Thinking errors can't survive the light. Thinking errors live in our unconscious brain, so they seem like observations, not deliberate choices. When we bring them forward to consciousness, the ones that don't serve us wither.

That all may sound good in theory, I hear you say, but how do we actually do that without ruining our reputations and our careers? That is a fair question, and it is important to be deliberate and strategic in the way we talk about and deal with sexual harassment. In this book, I explain the seven strategies I use in teaching my clients how to defend their careers from sexual harassment so that they can advance in fulfilling work. Those seven strategies are:

Strategy 1: Law. When women do not understand how the law applies to their particular situation (or whether it applies at all), they often accidentally do things that make it more difficult for the law to protect them. When a client comes to me, I first consider the law and help them understand how the law applies to their situation. Usually, this is somewhat simple. The most important thing to know about the law is that there are time limitations on any legal claim, so it is very important to have a lawyer evaluate how the law applies to your particular situation early so that you make sure you know all of your options.

I always tell my clients that the law only addresses a very narrow amount of wrong things, and it is very particular about the procedures it uses to address that narrow amount of wrong things. One of the biggest problems I see is women avoiding legal advice because most law offices are set up to file in court, rather than to help women actually address and end the harassment they are experiencing. There are often many steps women can take to end harassment before filing a lawsuit, though traditional law firms may not be equipped to teach them.

For some people, a lawsuit is the best option, though, and things have gone so far that a lawsuit is necessary. I always hope for my clients that a lawsuit does not become necessary, but if it does, I'm prepared. Juries, the courtroom, and litigation in general are incredibly fun when they are encountered with strength and love. A lawsuit, if it is necessary, can be something that shows you how strong you are.

In Chapter 3, I explain how to use the legal system in your favor.

Strategy 2: Reality. In many cases, either the law does not apply to a sexual harassment scenario or my clients want to deliberately choose a strategy that is contrary to what the law expects. I always tell them that it is better to defend your career and thrive in it than to have a good legal claim, and I wholeheartedly believe that. If every woman who consults with me could stop the harassment she is experiencing and thrive in her career, with no legal claim, I would be incredibly happy for them.

But, ending harassment and thriving is very different than ignoring harassment or backing down and justifying it. Ending harassment comes from a place of strength and love; ignoring or justifying it comes from a place of fear. With each of my clients, from accountants to lawyers to nurses to entrepreneurs, trusting their intuition (listening to their gut) is crucial to being successful in encountering harassment.

In encountering harassment, every person is unique in the realities of her situation and what will be best for her, her family, and her career. In Chapter 4, I explain why gut instinct is so important in countering harassment and how to develop that intuitive sense.

Strategy 3: Mapping. When clients come to me, they often have no plan for moving forward and feel stuck in what is happening to them. Either they think there is nothing they can do to end the harassment, or they have already quit a career and are unsure what their next step will be. I help my clients map out their next steps. In order to map out their next steps, I help them understand what they are thinking right now that gets them the results they have now and what they will need to think in order to create the results they want.

Now, it's easy to misunderstand this step and think that I am saying my clients' thoughts are drawing harassment to them. That is *not* what I'm saying. Your harasser's behavior is his own responsibility, and you did not cause it. And, your actions in how you respond are your responsibility and created by your thinking.

Many of us, when we experience harassment, make it mean incredibly cruel things about who we are and what we deserve. When our best friend experiences harassment, we know it says nothing negative about who she is and only negative things about her harasser. But, when it is about us, we stay stuck or confused because we are in a struggle with ourselves.

In Chapter 5, I teach you how to use your thinking and manage your feelings, so that they work in your favor to end harassment for good.

Strategy 4: Action. Many people feel stuck in indecision about whether they are really experiencing harassment and what they want for their lives, which keeps them from moving forward to create the life they want. I teach my clients how to be proactive, moving toward the life they want, rather than just reacting to what is happening around them. In creating the exact life you want, you have to honor and be deliberate about what you say "yes" to. I choose the word "yes" deliberately, in part because there is so much drama and stigma around the word "no." We try to teach girls how to say "no," and then we blame them for boys' behavior when they grow up and the boy doesn't listen. Then, those of us girls who have been in that position rebel against the unfair expectation that we have to say no and boys get to do whatever they want.

Don't put your brain on "no." Put your brain on "yes." Don't look toward what is unacceptable, but honor the enthusiastic, passionate, heart-pulling yesses in your life.

For every "yes" in your life, it represents many, many other things you are saying "no" to, and so each of your yesses is incredibly valuable.

Many of us were raised that it was our responsibility to take care of other people's feelings, and so our "yes" becomes people-pleasing instead of something valuable that we honor.

In Chapter 6, I teach you how to honor each of your "yesses," to start observing where you are willing to compromise your "yes," and to start to create the exact life you want.

Strategy 5: Consequences. When we are stuck in indecision about whether what we are experiencing is okay and arguing with ourselves about how to move forward, we usually make ourselves small and unconsciously make more space for harassment. We are so busy struggling with ourselves that we are basically rewarding the behavior we don't want. In order to get past that, I help my clients deliberately define their boundaries and set consequences for boundary violations.

I had a client tell me the other day, "I don't like the word 'boundaries.' It's so squishy." I had to agree with her. One time, I was reading a record of a conduct proceeding against a student who had been harassing his colleagues. The women who were bringing the case against him explained that they had tried to set boundaries and let him know it was not okay to touch them. "But, what if my boundary is to touch them?!" the man exclaimed in the hearing.

It's time to redefine boundaries (or at least get back to what boundaries really are). When we talk about boundaries in relationships, often we are not talking about boundaries at all – we are talking about our expectations for the other person's behavior (my boundary is for you to love me = not a boundary; my boundary is for you to be respectful = not a boundary). A boundary in relationships is really similar to a property boundary. It is a line of where you end and another person begins, and it is your job to respect and honor your own boundary.

When someone crosses the boundary, you are not helpless, just like you are not helpless if someone breaks into your home. A boundary is something for you to honor and respect in yourself and it is worth enforcing consequences when someone violates your boundaries. In Chapter 7, I teach you how to enforce consequences for sexual harassment that respect and honor you.

Strategy 6: Creation. Creating the exact life you want is the most effective form of resistance to harassment and discrimination. When we have experienced trauma, as most of my clients have, it becomes challenging to envision a healthy future for ourselves and impossible to envision the exact life we want. But, new research shows that some of the most dramatic creation can come from a traumatic event. Now, I'm not saying we need to go seek out traumatic events to create growth – life presents enough of those. I am saying that plants sprout from broken seeds; the lotus flower grows in the mud; the phoenix rises from the ashes; diamonds are made from incredible pressure on coal; pearls are made from sand irritating clams; and all of the other analogies you've probably heard a million times. If that is too abstract for you, what I am saying is this: I don't care where you are or what you have been through, you can use it to create something beautiful.

For someone to be diagnosed with post-traumatic stress disorder (PTSD), the psychiatry manual, *Diagnostic and Statistical Manual of Mental Disorders* (DSM-5), requires that she was exposed to a life-threatening, traumatic event. Many trauma researchers and practitioners who deal with trauma, however, dispute the usefulness of that requirement. Most, if not all, of us have experienced a life-threatening event. Beyond that, what each of us perceives as life-threatening is different.

I will say that when, early in my legal career, my boss was giving me back rubs, I perceived that as life-threatening. I had been in other situations where I had unwanted attention from men, but I had never been in a situation where I was "not supposed" to fight back. I had literally kicked people off of me in the past, but I knew that kicking my boss would risk my career.

It would not be appropriate to diagnose me with PTSD at this point in my life from that experience, and I am actually grateful (no joke, I'm not being squishy) to that boss for giving me an experience that taught me so much. But, at the point I was dealing with the harassment, I had many symptoms of PTSD.

We are tough; we are strong; but, sexual harassment takes a toll. It is important to understand how trauma can affect your brain and your body so that you can be fully informed in dealing with your own personal symptoms. In Chapter 8, I teach you about trauma, the growth that can come from trauma, and how to tap into your growth potential.

Strategy 7: Purpose. Choosing a purpose is key to creating the exact life you want. Viktor Frankl, in the life-changing book *Man's Search for Meaning*, described that Freud believed humans are motivated by pleasure, but Frankl believed we are actually motivated by meaning, and when we can't find meaning, it looks like we are motivated by pleasure.

I love that so much.

Often, when women consistently experience harassment, we absorb the discriminatory messages in culture, and we start to believe the cruel messages that we deserve less than men. This quickly becomes suicidal thinking and self-destructive behavior. We start to believe that we do not have a purpose or – if we do have one – we'll never find it.

It is important to remember that suicidal thinking and self-destructive behavior are not evidence that we are causing harassment or that we deserve harassment. Anyone who is harassing you is responsible for his own actions. I know that is easy to intellectually understand, but often, our subconscious confuses the two. When we mistakenly think harassment is our fault, or that we deserve it, we are on the side of our harassers, and we've abandoned ourselves.

Don't worry. You can come back to yourself.

The way to come back to yourself is to let go of judgment and decide what your purpose is. It's that simple, even though it may be hard work to practice your purpose. The hard work is so worth it. In Chapter 10, I teach you how to let go of self-destructive thinking and find purpose.

If you are struggling with whether your career is safe from harassment and sexism, the assessment, "Is Your Workplace Safe From Sexual Harassment?" is available at:

https://freedomresourcecenter.com/is-your-career-safe

Nothing in these chapters substitutes for having an individualized strategy created for you or having someone on your side who can help you manage this experience. But, these strategies give you an overview of the career defense trainings I offer, and the personalized strategizing I do for my VIP clients to help them overcome harassment and get the respect they deserve in their careers. As I said before, the most important lesson, which applies to each of these strategies, is to talk openly, deliberately, and strategically about any harassment you are experiencing and know there is no shame on you for someone else perpetrating harassment.

Chapter 3

———— ❋ ————

Strategy 1: Law

Whether or not you are asking in the back of your mind, "Do I have a legal case?" it will help you to have an understanding of what the law can do for you – and what it can't – in order to end harassment in your life for good. Because I don't know your story, and I may not work in your state, this is not legal advice. This is a very, very rough description of how the law works federally and in many states and what it protects. Protections around discrimination are different from state to state and country to country, so it is very important to talk to a local attorney about how the law applies to your situation before you do anything that might affect a legal claim. I want what I'm telling you to help you and not hurt you, so *please* take this seriously.

If you don't know a local attorney, *I will find one for you.* That is how seriously I take this. Just send me an email at Meredith@ FreedomResourceCenter.com, include a very brief description of what is going on with you, and let me know where you live. If I can't help you, I will help you find someone who can.

Criminal Versus Civil

The law is broken up into two parts: criminal and civil. Criminal law deals with people's freedom. If you break a criminal law, you could go to jail or have a probation officer follow you around.

Civil law deals almost exclusively with money. In very rare cases, civil law can provide something other than money to repair the wrong that happened, but for purposes of this rough understanding of the law, you should assume civil law only deals with money.

For example, imagine two neighbors have a dispute because the one neighbor drove over the other's lawn and damaged the landscaping. On the criminal side, the police might investigate whether the offending neighbor intentionally trespassed or was driving while intoxicated (violations of criminal law). If the police and the district attorney's office decided that the offending neighbor broke a criminal law, the DA would then decide whether to go to court to try to restrict the offending neighbor's freedom (send her to jail) as punishment or put the offending neighbor in some kind of program to rehabilitate her and help her contribute positively to society. The purpose of that system is to protect the community from the offender and (hopefully sometimes) to rehabilitate the offender to society. It does not focus on helping the hurt person.

On the civil side, the hurt neighbor could decide whether to ask for some kind of reparation for the harm to the lawn. If the offending neighbor wouldn't agree to a reparation, the hurt neighbor could file a lawsuit. A judge and jury might order the offending neighbor to pay the estimated cost of repairing the landscaping. A judge and jury would usually not be allowed to order the offending neighbor to physically repair the landscaping herself, though. One of the reasons is that it is way easier to enforce the transfer of money than to make sure the neighbor does a good job repairing the landscape. No one wants the judge to go stand over the neighbor and watch her plant shrubs to make sure it gets done. We want the hurt neighbor to be able to decide what landscaping to get, but the offending neighbor to still be responsible to pay for it.

I am going to come back to this analogy of a neighbor driving over another neighbor's lawn – not with any intent of being disrespectful by comparing it to how it can feel to be harassed or assaulted. But, in terms of the law, I think comparing the two can be helpful, and it is often less triggering to talk about a damaged lawn than harassment or assault.

But, now I am going to apply this analogy to the ways that harassment and assault cases can play out in the criminal and civil law, so be conscious of yourself and where you are when you read this. Read in a safe space, where you feel comfortable that you can put this book down and do something comforting if you start feeling overwhelmed. The information will be here when you get back. If you force yourself to learn this when you are not ready to receive it, it will not be helpful to you.

Also, feel free at any time to skip this chapter and go right to the next. If you know you are not planning to make a legal claim or you have an attorney to give you legal advice, then you do not need to put yourself through this chapter, which may just be more boring than triggering.

For those of you still around, I'm here for ya.

The law only gets involved with a very, very narrow selection of harms – especially for women. The law changes very slowly, and there are still not enough women in government to create strong representation of women's perspectives. We have a situation where the law was written by men. So, as with health insurance paying for Viagra but not birth control, the law is usually very specific about how it addresses traditionally male concerns, but it doesn't do a lot for women. We also have a situation where we have a culture traditionally ashamed of anything to do with sex. So, even though men experience harassment, too, they may feel even more cultural pressure than women to pretend it doesn't exist.

Below are specifics about how the law addresses harassment scenarios at home, work, or in the community. I do not address how the law handles cyber situations because it provides little to no protection in those situations. In many cyber instances, it actually provides more protection for the harasser than the harassed, but as with everything, there are always other strategies you can use to deal with harassment. You are not stuck. Again, this is not legal advice because I don't know how this information applies to you specifically, but instead is meant to be practical information to be aware of what exists in the law.

Police

My experience with criminal law is from working in our Oregon state court and working with the police and district attorney's office to coordinate with the criminal side of civil cases. So, take it for what it is worth in terms of how it applies to your local system.

No one is allowed to touch your body without your permission. Sometimes, if someone touches your body without your permission, it is a crime. Usually, but not always, if the harassment you experience does not involve harm to your body or your property, it would not fall under criminal law. Again, it is important to talk to an attorney or the police about how the law applies to your particular experience.

In criminal law, the presumption is that the perpetrator of the crime is innocent, unless the government proves he is guilty (say it with me, *Law & Order* fans) "beyond a reasonable doubt." If there is any reasonable doubt about the perpetrator's innocence, the jury can't convict him.

This is meant to be a high standard to keep the government from putting innocent people in prison. The problem is that it is usually very, very difficult to prove crimes against women beyond a reasonable doubt. Women often experience crimes in our homes or our workplaces when alone with perpetrators who are people we trust. No one sees what we experience, and our perpetrators lie if someone asks them what happened. If there is not a third-party witness, clear forensic evidence, or video or written evidence of some kind of confession, juries often feel they can find reasonable doubt as to the guilt of the defendant. A major pitfall I see in these situations is that people think recording their perpetrator confessing on audio will help – these recordings are sometimes a crime and usually not admissible in court, so be very careful if you are thinking about doing that.

The law was written by men in a culture that shames sexuality. It is only within the last 50 years that we have started to expect the police to arrest people for crimes committed between intimate partners.

The standards we have now, especially on the criminal side, only allow the police to intervene when something has gone very, very wrong. They put the burden on women who are being harassed to clearly say no, fight back, and defend ourselves. If this is not a realistic solution in your case, Chapter 4 is for you.

In order to help with the problem that the criminal law is not set up to keep women safe, police often recommend that women who are being harassed get restraining or stalking orders.

Restraining Orders

Sometimes, restraining orders are a good idea. If you have children with someone who is violent, sometimes it is necessary to take out a restraining order to have an emergency custody plan for the children. Other times, a court order can be appropriate if you have no relationship with your harasser. For example, I worked with a client who was a college instructor, and one of her students was threatening her because she did not want to date him. He made explicit physical threats, but also, he sent her super creepy emails all the time. Because she was eligible for a stalking order based on some of his conduct, each one of the emails he sent after the stalking order was in place became a crime, and her stalker actually faced criminal sanctions for them.

That situation is the exception, in my experience. In *The Gift of Fear*, Gavin de Becker recommends women be very careful before we file for stalking or restraining orders, and I have to agree with him. Often court orders can escalate violence because they put someone unstable into a threatening situation, where he feels undermined and ridiculed by society. The judge tells him not to contact someone again, and he suddenly needs to prove he has ownership over the woman he's not supposed to contact. Unfortunately, women have been kidnapped or killed after filing for restraining orders.

A more common problem than escalating physical violence, though, is the problem of wanting to have ongoing contact. For example, I worked with a professional artist who was dating a violent, unstable man. At first, their relationship was exciting, but it soon turned co-dependent and dangerous. He threatened her life and her friends' property. He physically hurt her and destroyed her belongings. But, because of her own story about him and about herself, she went back to him over and over again. At one point, she wanted to get a restraining order against him, not just to keep him away, but to keep herself from going back to him. But, that's not how these orders work. A stalking, restraining, or protective order almost always restrains the perpetrator only.

What often happens in scenarios like that is the woman gets an order, but she hasn't let go of the story that draws her back to the perpetrator, and so she goes back to him. She either dismisses the restraining order or gets the man to violate it. Then, he is violent again, and she calls the police, saying that the restraining order is violated. When he goes to court for the violation of the restraining order, his attorney undermines the woman's credibility – after all, she went back to the perpetrator. She is just using the restraining order as a bargaining tool with the perpetrator, the attorney argues. She does not really believe she is in danger or she wouldn't have gone back to him.

The law assumes everyone acts in his own best interest. I don't know if I've mentioned this enough yet, but it was written by men in a culture that shames people around sex.

The worst-case scenario in that situation is that the man commits a horrible crime against the woman, but she has already been shown to be not credible in court, so the government can't prosecute and the man walks free. Unfortunately, this is not uncommon.

When I worked at my local courthouse, just out of law school, I walked the two miles to work and home. My friends would tell me not to walk in the dark and that it was dangerous to be out walking after work. Some of them would wait for me to be done with court to drive me home on a dark night.

From everything we saw in court, I knew I was not the one in danger. While I worked there, I saw zero cases of stranger attacks, but almost every day of the week, I saw cases of "Assault – Domestic Violence," "Strangulation," and "Interference with a Report." The stories were almost all the same: a man hit his partner, she reached for her cell phone to call the police, and he slammed her up against the wall with his hands to her throat, throwing the phone across the room. These charges came through the courthouse almost every single day.

Men are one of the leading sources of injury and death in women around the world. These are usually the men we work with, live with, and rely on, though – not strangers. This violence is a disease that is part of our communities and needs a cure. The amputation idea of restraining orders and jail isn't working. Cutting off men from their victims for a little while is not a long-term solution.

When the artist I worked with came to me, we worked together on a step-by-step intervention that allowed her to remove herself from the toxic relationship as she was ready. She is now safe and away from that relationship. She is still processing her own thoughts, trauma, and how to plan for her safety, but she is out of immediate danger. We started with just practicing calling the police when she was in danger. If you are not able to get yourself into the mindset that you can call the police to protect yourself without a restraining order, it is unlikely that the restraining order itself will change that. You need to be able to call the police when you are in danger, with or without a restraining order.

In her particular situation, she needed to move to a different city in order to remove herself from her perpetrator's control. Moving is not always the best option, and I prefer to help people get to a position where they can stay where they are and defend their lives from the harassment, forcing the harasser to move or stop instead. But, if moving is a realistic way to protect yourself from physical danger, there is no shame in it.

Once she moved, though, the man still would not leave her alone, and so we sent a cease-and-desist letter. A cease-and-desist letter is sometimes an appropriate substitute for a restraining or stalking order. The cease and desist provides written proof that you have told the perpetrator not to contact you, but it does not require the court process of a restraining order. Because it is still a formal letter, it is important that you have committed to not interacting with the perpetrator anymore at the time you send the cease and desist, but if you do end up seeing the perpetrator again, it does not have the same power to undermine your credibility. On average, people return to abusive situations between 8 and 16 times. It is important to have a flexible approach to training yourself to set boundaries around harassment and violence. Calling the police, leaving, and cease and desist letters can all be appropriate steps in that process.

A sample copy of a cease and desist letter is included as Appendix I. Please talk to an attorney in your area before you send this so that you understand the impact that it could have on any legal (criminal or civil) case. I'm happy to talk to you about your situation, see if I can help, and connect you to someone in your area, as well (Meredith@ FreedomResourceCenter.com).

Civil Claims

Basically, civil rights law makes it illegal for the government to discriminate based on certain protected characteristics. It also makes it illegal for some employers to discriminate against some employees and sometimes customers. Sex is almost always a protected characteristic, though it gets less protection than race under some legal analyses.

I'll say it again, though, to make sure I was clear. These are the people who aren't allowed to discriminate: the government, employers (against employees), and sometimes businesses against their customers.

Otherwise, it's a free-for-all, and you may not be protected against discrimination or most forms of harassment. What I'm talking about now is different than what we talk about as a "hate crime" – crimes are still crimes, and if they are motivated by discrimination, there may be stricter punishments for them. What I'm talking about now is discriminatory attitudes and conduct that don't seriously injure someone's body or their property. The good news is that this does not mean you are out of luck (as I'll talk about in future chapters), but it may mean the law does not protect you. It also may mean that even if the law technically prohibits what you're experiencing, it doesn't actually protect you in reality.

For example, commonly, there is no civil recourse in intimate partner violence or harassment. The reason for this is that even if the violence is illegal (which it is), your harasser's liability insurance (if he has it) almost certainly does not cover violence, harassment, or any other intentional harm. If you think about it, this makes some theoretical sense, even though it screws you – we don't want to have men buying insurance because they plan to beat up their partner. But, in reality, it is just a scheme that helps insurance companies and hurts people who are the most seriously injured.

Sometimes, a perpetrator has his own money and assets, and you are able to file a lawsuit to recover against those. This is tricky, because individuals can transfer their assets to trusts or business entities, and that makes it very difficult to actually recover anything. Sometimes, you can garnish wages, but again that can be tricky, and anything you do to chase your perpetrator's money keeps you tied to him in a way that I won't support.

Unfortunately, the next thing to know is that even if the person harassing you is the government, your employer, or a business owner, you still might not be protected, depending on their behavior and how you respond to it.

Generally, in order for the law to protect you against harassment, it has to have been (1) unwanted, (2) offensive to a reasonable person in your situation, and (3) severe or pervasive. You have to have alerted your employer to the harassment or, if you are being harassed by your supervisor, you have to have taken advantage of whatever reporting options are available. If there are no reporting options or your harasser is the owner of the company, you may be relieved of this expectation in some ways. Then, if you report, and your employer does not respond promptly and effectively, you may have a legal claim. If you report and get fired or demoted, or some other significant privilege taken away, you may have a legal claim. If your boss wants you to have sex with him, you say no, and he takes away some privilege of your job, you may have a legal claim.

You may be able to tell that the law assumes that the women it is protecting are low-level employees. When it was written, women were barely allowed to work in paying jobs, and so the concept was just to minimize some of the obstacles to women keeping their low-level jobs. As women go further and further up in their profession, even as they become entrepreneurs, this system becomes less and less realistic as a protection against harassment. If you own your company, and you have a competitor, colleague, or even ex-boyfriend harassing, threatening, and demeaning you, who are you supposed to report to? You are the boss. The law expects you, as the top-level player, to have an equal playing ground as the men in your field. That is not always realistic, and so, as with everything you've done to get where you are, you will need more strategies and support than your male counterparts. It's not pretty, but it's reality.

Tips for Reporting

If you are in a position where you have someone you can report to, I encourage you to follow up on your report in writing. What I usually see as most successful is reporting to an ally in a superior position in person. So, go to his or her office, sit down, and explain what's happening. Make it clear that the harassment is unwanted, offensive, and severe or pervasive. If it is not any of those things yet, and you want to address the harassment before it gets worse, just make it clear why you think you are being harassed or experiencing discrimination. Sit with yourself before this meeting, and be clear with yourself about why you think you are being harassed or experiencing discrimination. A lot of times, we "just know" something is discriminatory, even if it is not explicit, but if we really think about why we "just know," we can come up with a more specific reason than that. When you have the meeting, be open to other interpretations of what is going on. Consider the other interpretations, and if they don't ring true to you, listen to your own intuition about why.

Then, follow up with your report in writing. I recommend following up with an email, and I am including a sample email as Appendix II. Make sure the email is in your words, but be clear about the harassment you are experiencing and that it needs to stop.

Unfortunately, if you quit your job, it makes a legal claim much more difficult to pursue. The law on the civil side, like the law on the criminal side, expects women to fight for themselves, even when that is an unrealistic expectation.

If the harassment does not stop, making a legal claim is one way to continue to enforce your boundaries. Like with the example of the two neighbors and the ruined lawn, harassment that rises to the level of a legal claim is a boundary violation. Your physical integrity and emotional integrity are boundaries that no one is allowed to violate. If someone violates them, there are consequences. The law provides consequences for some of those violations, but not all of them. You can still set other consequences, and Chapter 7 talks about that more thoroughly.

When you have been in a harassing situation for a while, it can feel natural to expect bad things and even to turn to self-harm. Sometimes, then, when you're trying to get out of a situation, the legal system can become another form of self-harm. If that idea raises a tickle in your brain or makes you squirm because you think it might be true of you, go to Chapter 5 and consider tools for managing your thinking around your harassment and trauma. None of this means something is wrong with you. It is totally normal stuff that our brains do. It is easy to use the legal system as a new perpetrator, to take your harasser's place, and I would rather see you succeed and overcome what you've been through. I know you can do it. You have support.

If you don't think the law applies to your situation or you don't want to use the law, don't worry. You are not out of luck. There are many, many practical and reality-based strategies for ending harassment. The law is only one, limited strategy for defending your career.

Chapter 4

_____ ✲ _____

Strategy 2: Reality

I am writing this chapter on the most beautiful rainy day. I wish you could be here with me. I woke up early, meditated, wrote in my journal, and planned my day. When my cat, Cressida, wanted to go outside, I opened the door, and I could hear the shower of rain coming down in the parking lot. I coached a client, and then I took a walk. On my walk, it was sunny and beautiful. The path was shimmering with sunlight, and the sky was pale winter blue. I talked with my best friend, Erica, on my walk, and she helped me work out some legal puzzles for a client. Now, I am lying on my couch and the storm is knocking at my door. Outside the rain is pouring in a slant over my house and the trees are swaying in the wind. The laundry machine is swishing water, and I am so comfortable.

I do want to give you some clarity about how to defend your career against sexual harassment, though, and not just lie here so cozy in the rain. I remember that when the harassment I was experiencing was at its most extreme, I lost all ability to even appreciate a warm house on a rainy day. My entire body was consumed with fear about harassment and despair about who I was and what I deserved. I was afraid all the time. Understanding the law and how it applied to my situation was no help in reducing my fear – instead, it added a level of pressure and confusion because it is impossible to get a straight answer about how the law applies. I was afraid I would do something wrong and ruin any legal claim I might have and I was afraid a legal claim would ruin my career. I wanted to talk about what I was experiencing, but I thought it made people too uncomfortable and they couldn't help me anyway.

I know you are strong enough to experience the fear and stress you are under right now, but I also know your experience does not have to stay as stressful and terrifying as it is now. You can feel better and you can deal with harassment in the way that is right for you, no matter how the law applies.

It can feel very disempowering to hear about how narrow the legal prohibitions against discrimination and harassment are and how little the law will do to protect you when you are being harassed.

It can be easy to give up at that point. Every year, women lose hundreds of thousands of dollars in their careers because the law doesn't protect them from harassment and they don't know what to do next. Those women avoid promotions, take demotions, or leave their jobs for lower paying jobs to get away from their harassers. Polling shows that one in four women has left a career because of harassment.

And no one would blame them. You never need to put up with harassment. You do not owe that to yourself or to anyone else. Leaving is always an option. But, often if you quit, you lose legal protection, and also, you miss out on a huge opportunity to understand your life and grow in it.

Particularly where kids are involved, moms often look at this as an excruciating choice between the frying pan and the fire. Before they come to me, my clients often think their only choices are between staying in an abusive job (and feeding their children) or leaving (and letting their children starve or sending them to live with grandma). I want better than that for you, and your kids definitely deserve better. The truth is that there *are* other options.

So how do you figure out the reality of what you should do?

Identify the Problem Behavior

First, be very clear about what the harassing behavior is. Be very specific. What was said? What was done?

If you want to protect yourself or preserve a legal claim, reflect on whether your harassment is based on your race, gender, religion, or another protected characteristic (check with an attorney in your state to find out what characteristics are protected). What I see most commonly with my clients is that they know they are being targeted because they are women, but they would rather point to any other reason when they're talking about it. They would rather say, "He was mad that I paid for his lunch" than "He hates women and tries to put them in their place."

I think this happens because we think it is "bad" or somehow morally wrong, rather than just incorrect, for people to demonstrate sexism. Then, we think that if we are identifying sexism, it's going to look judgmental. This creates the really unhelpful situation where we are inaccurately talking about sexism in a way that makes sure it will never change.

The motivation for the harassment is separate from identifying the problem behavior, but still important. Problem behavior is something like, "He touched my shoulder" or "He said, 'Stop talking.'" The motivation is something like, "I think he is threatened by women because he only talks to women that way," or "I think he's hangry because he acts like that when he hasn't had lunch."

Sexism is prohibited by the law. Hangriness is not prohibited by the law. So, after you have identified the problem behavior, it is somewhat important to figure out what you think is motivating the problem behavior and why you think that. Our brains often signal suspicion when we think behavior is sexist, but sometimes it also creates a huge barrier against identifying that motivation.

For example, I consulted with a top manager for a research non-profit, who was being laid off. Her research line was being cut, and she was suspicious that it was because she was a woman. When I first asked her why she thought that, she couldn't put her finger on it, and she mentioned that maybe she was just being overly sensitive.

I say to women in those situations that when we think something is sexist, there is usually a good reason if we can let ourselves be curious about it and pull the reason out of our memory. Once we have done that, we can address it. If we let it remain a suspicion in our unconscious, we can't do anything about it.

After I gave her some space to think about why, she had many reasons. She explained that she was on a project a year earlier, and she was the only one who was removed from the project. She was also the only woman on the project. The man who organized the project, the head of their non-profit, was notoriously sexist, but no one would complain about it because they were afraid for their jobs. She gave me other examples of sexism women talked about behind his back. She had never raised any issues regarding sexism, but now her research line was the only one being cut. It seemed like retribution for the ways she had questioned him when they worked on the project. Those examples were not at the forefront of her memory because she was not looking for sexism in her job. But, she was able to retrieve them when she took the time to be curious.

I worked with a lawyer recently who was questioned in an investigation regarding sexism in her firm. She explained to me that she thought the male partners' attitude to women was not "sexist," but was "authoritarian," which she also believed was a problem.

The important thing to know is that it is not illegal to be authoritarian, hangry, or even cruel, but it is illegal to be sexist in a work environment.

Most people don't care if someone was authoritarian or even mean to you. I'm sorry to say that, but they don't. On the other hand, as a society, we have come more and more to recognize that targeting people based on immutable characteristics is stupid and unhelpful, so we're doing slightly more to change that.

Authoritarianism and bad leadership are probably a problem in any sexist environment you are in, but if you want your environment to change, you need to be really deliberate about what you want to change. It is also most effective in making change when you are willing to be accurate and use the tools available to you (like the law) in your favor. If you want to encourage your harasser to grow in his leadership skills, that might be worth it to you, and there are many great books about leadership. Because you are reading this book, I think you want your harasser to stop targeting you as a woman. If you implement the strategies in this book, one of the side effects may be that your harasser is forced to have better leadership skills and be accountable for his crappy leadership skills, but that is not the purpose of any of these strategies.

If you are trying to address leadership skills in the same conversation where you are addressing sexual harassment, your harasser is not going to get it. If you are telling someone else (police, a reporting agency, or even your friend) about bad leadership skills in the same conversation where you want to report sexual harassment, they are going to think you and your harasser just have a personality conflict that you can deal with yourselves.

No one wants to get involved in a personality conflict. Some people are required to respond to sexual harassment.

Be really clear in your own mind whether what you are experiencing is based in sexism or based in something else. It may be for you that, like the lawyer I was working with, you genuinely believe your environment is not sexist, but is authoritarian. Just knowing that could be helpful in understanding what you can do to effectively make change. Sometimes, it is even a relief to understand that a bad leader is mean to everyone, not just women. Whatever your results are, it is important to take some time and be curious about the exact problem behavior, what you believe motivates it, and why you believe that.

When we are uncomfortable about identifying sexism and we are more comfortable staying in that unconscious suspicious place, it is almost always because of extreme thoughts we have about sexism. What I typically see is that those thoughts are something like a combination of, "Maybe I do actually deserve disrespect," "I don't want to be a victim," and "If I say anything about this, it will ruin his life."

We can usually see that those thoughts are nonsense when they're written down, and we would not say them to anyone else, but they are very, very typical. Our brain tries to find any other reason for what we're experiencing because of our thoughts around what it would mean to experience sexism.

But, we can't do anything to change something that we're not willing to even consider. There is nothing we can do to overcome sexism in our lives if we're not willing to acknowledge it exists.

Not all meanness we experience is based in sexism, but when we close our eyes to the sexism around us, it leaves us powerless victims to that very sexism.

So, in this first step of this strategy, we identify the problem behavior and what we think is motivating it. This step is like when you go to the mall, and you know you need to go to Banana Republic, so you walk up to the sign that shows the map of the store. The map shows the star that says "You Are Here." You need to find the "You Are Here" star before you can figure out how to get to Banana. Being clear on the harassment you are experiencing and whether it is based in discrimination is finding that star.

Build Support

The next thing to do is to identify the allies around you that will support you. You don't need to build a formal group or have meetings or anything, but just be specific about the people around you whose opinions you trust and who do provide support. Even if your list only includes your cat, put her on there. An ally is someone you can tell about your experience and get realistic feedback and perspective from *or* someone who supports you no matter what. It's not necessarily someone who agrees with you (although it can be), but it is someone whose opinion you respect and someone who will give their opinion with respect to you. It is okay for your support group to include people who also are just going to agree with you no matter what. The purpose of this group isn't to question your perspective (although that could be a helpful side effect), it is to remind yourself that there are people who respect you.

When you are identifying your support group, you don't need to tell them your story, although you can. The first step, though, is just figuring out where you are and who supports you.

If you can't think of anyone else to put on your list, that is not a crisis, and it happens quite often. It is just information for you to know. Go ahead and put me on your list because I absolutely support you. And then be curious about whether it could be possible in the future to find one other person who supports you. I'll give you the answer: it is completely possible.

Identifying allies and building support can be crucial to overcoming harassment. In my experience with sexual harassment early in my career, as I talked about earlier, I was working in a professional setting, and my colleague, who was in a higher position than me, would give me back rubs, lean his body against me, and comment on my clothing and appearance. He told me I was more important than his wife, although he and I were only vaguely acquainted and had only talked in a professional setting, and he brought up not knowing how I tasted. It was super gross. I reported the harassment to four different people before someone finally made him apologize to me and stop. As I reported, though, I built allies. Almost every person I told agreed with me that the harassment needed to stop and collaborated with me about how to make that happen. When I mentioned it to someone who made it clear she did not understand, I stopped discussing it with her.

Sometimes you have to let people go when they are not going to support you in moving forward and overcoming harassment. This does not mean silencing yourself. It just means that the purpose of talking about the harassment is not to make sure everyone likes you or to create a group of hall monitors who can tell you what you are doing wrong. The purpose is to find the group that wants to walk with you in what you are experiencing. You are not alone, and you don't have to figure this out on your own.

Whether or not you choose to report the harassment, it is important to realize there are people on your side.

This lets you build safety. We often put off building our own safety because we think we can't feel safe until the harassment stops. This is not true and it actually clouds our judgment and makes us less safe. It puts power over our safety in our harasser's hands. Building your own safety-and-support system gives you the power back and it reminds you that you never need to tolerate behavior that you don't want. There are people on your side.

It is also important because harassment can be physically dangerous. Even when harassment starts out in a mild way – someone you work with pays a little too much attention to your clothes, for example – it can escalate. In *Why Does He Do That*, Lundy Bancroft, a counselor who worked with men who were convicted of abuse against women, describes the psychology of sexist behavior in men. He makes this brilliant analogy that basically goes like this:

A young man is told by his family he will inherit property when he comes of age. Finally, he comes of age and goes to his property to claim it. When he gets there, people tell him it is a public park. He argues with them, and they show him the city's deed to the park. He goes back to his family, who confirm that it is actually his. This argument with the townspeople goes on for quite some time, but ultimately, he moves into the park, and he tells the town he will designate a small portion as a park. That doesn't work for the townspeople, who know the whole thing is actually a park. The man starts threatening the townspeople and buys guns to shoot them if they enter the park because it's the only recourse he has left to defend what's his.

I love that analogy so much. Many men are raised, whether overtly or subtly, that women's bodies and lives belong to them. This raising happens in the commercials on TV, in school when boys' answers are praised and girls' answers are criticized, and when boys are allowed to walk outside at night while girls are confined to their homes. There are so many ways we train boys with this message.

That in no way justifies abusive behavior. But, raising boys with that sense of entitlement can be physically dangerous.

Building a team of allies who support you creates safety against that entitlement. The people you designate as allies are like the town reaching out to neighboring towns for support to get the entitled man off of the property. I'm kind of sorry for the way referring to your space as literal property crosses over to the outdated idea of women as property or objects. But, I hope you can see here that your space, and your right to your own bodily and emotional integrity, are your property. You are not the property, but just because you are human, you are the town that owns the property. You deserve your own space, and no one is entitled to control you. Surround yourself with people who understand that and support you.

This step is like your trip to the mall, when you've gone with some friends. You know you want to go to Banana Republic, but some of your friends want to go to JC Penney and others want to go to Macy's. This step is identifying who wants to go to Banana with you.

Trust Your Instincts

Women are often made fun of for their "women's intuition" while men are trusted for their "gut instinct." In *The Gift of Fear*, Gavin de Becker describes that, when he is performing a threat assessment, the dangerous person almost always turns out to be the person that the woman describes saying, "It couldn't be this person, but there was this weird thing...." Research shows that the only reliable way to know if a woman is in physical danger from a harassment threat is whether she thinks she is.

The majority of thoughts we have happen in the unconscious level. For example, our brains show activity when we walk, but we are not consciously thinking, "Pick up my left foot, move it forward, now put it down." We did have those thoughts when we were learning to walk (though probably not using the words "left" and "right" unless we were re-learning to walk as adults), but at this point, all of that has been moved to our unconscious.

Our brains developed so that their primary task is saving our lives, and that task lives on the unconscious level. This unconscious thinking is usually what we refer to as intuition or gut instinct. Interestingly, there is a network of neurons, or brain cells, in our digestive system, which is sometimes called the "little brain." So when we identify our motivation as coming from our gut, it is often literally true.

When you have an intuitive sense of danger, often what is happening is that your brain is processing the danger on an unconscious level, and if you consciously look back later, you can piece out what exactly signaled you.

Trust your intuition. It will save your life.

What messes us up is that when we experience consistent harassment, we go into a state of constant fear that dulls our intuition. Constant fear is not intuition. Our intuition about danger is the unconscious, animal part of our brain that senses a predator. Constant fear comes from the stories we tell ourselves about what we deserve and who we are.

When we start developing a support team of allies, often what we want to do is start looking to them for all of our answers about what we should do and whether we're right about our harassment. When we start to look to other people for what we should do, we lose our path.

You are the leader of your own life. Come back to yourself and your own intuition if you get off track and start to look to everyone else's opinion.

You are the leader of your own life. You have the best knowledge and insight into what is going on in your life.

Looking to other people's opinions is like deciding you want to follow everyone to Macy's and JC Penney rather than going to Banana Republic. You are on your own path, and your people will come with you.

Do the Math

Considering your own personal reality usually brings on a lot of confusion and helplessness. "Who do I listen to? Everyone has different opinions." "What will people think of me?" "I can't do anything to stop this." "What did I do to cause this?" "This is too embarrassing to talk about." Our brains spin out, keeping us stuck in fear.

In every situation, there is drama and there is math. Now, if you're like me, you love drama and hate math, so the instruction to "do the math" might sound terrible.

But, indulging in drama like the thoughts above keeps you stuck in fear. Your primitive, unconscious brain wants you to be stuck in fear because it is designed to conserve energy. If you are stuck in fear, hiding in a cave, you will not get eaten by a tiger. Your automatic brain can't tell the difference from harassment and a hungry tiger. It is supposed to keep you alive by triggering your nervous system to fight or flee when you run into danger. When we experience trauma consistently enough, our bodies start to freeze in reaction to it, not knowing whether to fight or flee. Nothing has gone wrong with you or with your body's response if you are feeling fear all the time and if you feel stuck in a thinking spiral of self-criticism and despair. Your brain is creating drama because it believes that will keep you safe like it kept your ancestors safe.

The good news is that your conscious brain can train your unconscious to do something different and more helpful. You do not need to feel fear all the time, and it is probably not actually protecting you from anything. The best way to make this shift is by doing the math – literally and figuratively. Literally, science shows that when you count backwards (even just from the number 5 – "5, 4, 3, 2, 1, liftoff") it wakes up your frontal lobe and you are better able to make decisions. (Mel Robbins, a former attorney, bases her practice on this simple technique, which she calls the "5 Second Rule.") If your brain is tangling you up into drama, simply counting backwards, or calculating your income for the year, or doing any math can take you out of your primitive brain's crisis.

Figuratively, doing the math just means getting back in touch with anything that feels neutral. You will make your best decisions if you can find something that is neutral about your situation. If you are making decisions from a place of crisis, you will reject about 90% of your viable options and you will be moving toward more crisis.

This is because our brains also do not process negative statements. As lawyers, we get a lot of training and admonishment about this for dealing with juries. So, if I'm presenting a case to a jury, and I say to them, "Don't hold it against my client that she quit her job," the jurors' brains will edit out the word "don't" and hear, "Hold it against my client."

All of our brains work like that, and so if you are spending most of your day thinking, "I don't want to make a mistake," your brain will be focused on mistakes. If you are thinking, "I don't want him to touch me," your brain will be focused on him touching you. In that scenario, you are at least devoting a lot of your energy to your harasser if not moving yourself toward situations that let you debate that thought.

We debate or negotiate a thought when we go back and forth between two extremes like, "I don't want him to touch me" and "Stop thinking about it, he's not going to touch you." What I mean is that if you are thinking about puppies, and negotiating whether you want or don't want a puppy, you might google puppies on the internet or go visit your friend who got a puppy. If you are thinking about harassment, you are not thinking about puppies at the same time. We have around 60,000 thoughts a day, but research on multitasking has shown that our brains can only hold one concept at a time. The more consumed we get with thinking about harassment, the less space we have for anything else.

Now, I want you to hear me clearly on this because it is really easy to misunderstand at this point, and I'm going to repeat this all the time to make sure you hear me. You are not responsible for your harasser's behavior. There is nothing you could think or say that would make you responsible for another person's behavior. I take that back – maybe if you were holding him at gunpoint, you would have some responsibility. I'm going to assume that you are not currently holding your harasser at gunpoint, forcing him to harass you, while reading this book. But, if you are doing that, I kind of want to say congratulations because that sounds both hard and weird. It also sounds like a waste of time, though, so you should stop and get on with your day.

Anyway, that does not mean you are powerless. You do not have power over your harasser's behavior, but you do have power over what you are thinking, how you are feeling, and what you do. There are thousands of responses we can have to harassment, and there are even thousands of *reasonable* responses we can have to harassment. You have control over your response.

To continue with the mall analogy, doing the drama is like standing at the "you are here" sign and wavering about what store you need to go to. Doing the math is like looking at your budget and your schedule, and making a decision to go to the store that works for you.

Talk with an Open Heart

Talk about your experience and be open to other perspectives. Like we talked about in Chapter 2, talking about your perspective is the most important way to make change. Be open to other people disagreeing with you, but stick to your perspective if theirs rings false. Talk about your experience of sexual harassment as if talking about it is a gift to your listener. It is.

If you lived in a time where doctors didn't wash their hands routinely, would you be grateful to someone who talked about the hygienic doctors and the unhygienic ones? Yes. Unless you wanted to die young, you would be grateful. No matter how uncomfortable people get at you talking about your experience, it is still a gift from you to them.

Talking about your experience is not like going to the mall. Sometimes it is like being burned with fire brands or having your skin scraped off. But, it is worth it, and the kindness and love that you give yourself and others in being willing to own your experience is worth the pain. In developing a personalized strategy to defend your career against sexual harassment, it is important to identify the problem behavior, build support, trust your instincts, and talk with an open heart.

ACTION STEPS:

Each of these steps is intended to prepare you to talk with an attorney if you choose to do so, and so it should be protected under attorney-client privilege. This book does not make me your attorney, but you can use these notes to help any attorney if you choose to talk with one. Keep in mind that if you keep a journal, calendar, or anything else written down (text messages, emails, social media messages, etc.), those are not confidential and can be turned over to your harasser if you bring a claim. If you keep a journal of your harassment and how it has affected you in order to prepare you to talk with an attorney, make sure it is clear in the journal that you are writing notes to prepare to talk with an attorney.

I have created a Personal Career Defense Toolkit for you, where you can fill these questions out yourself or you can create a notebook of your own and copy these questions into the notebook. Email me at Meredith@ FreedomResourceCenter.com to get a copy of the Personal Career Defense Toolkit. Include "Toolkit" in the subject line of your email.

Make sure that wherever you write this, it includes a notice that what you write is in anticipation of talking with an attorney and pursuing a legal claim. That means it should be attorney-client or work-product privileged. Talk with an attorney in your state to get the details of what that means. This is to prepare you to talk with an attorney:

1. Make a list of the particular problem behaviors that you are concerned about. Be as specific as possible.
2. Write down what you believe is motivating these behaviors (use no more than 5 words).
3. List seven allies you can access to build support.
4. Write down what your intuition tells you about what your next step should be. Remember, your intuition can recognize

a danger, but it is different than pervasive fear that keeps you stuck. What is the first thing that comes to mind?

5. What does the math look like for you? (What is the neutral reality of your circumstances now and what would you like your circumstances to be in the future?)

6. What do you want to say to people when you talk about the harassment you are experiencing?

7. How do you want to react if they have a negative response?

Chapter 5

———— 🌟 ————

Strategy 3: Mapping

When I create a personalized career defense plan with my VIP clients, one of the most important steps we take is to map out the results they want to get and what they need to do to get those results. When mountain climbers plan a huge climb or when Olympic athletes train for a major competition, they know that mapping out their results not only means specifically envisioning what they want, but it also means training their minds to think like the person who got those results.

I hate all the garbage ideas that if people are homeless or poor or victims of crimes, they somehow did something wrong to deserve it or there is something wrong with them. I think you see this kind of fake "positive thinking" and "law of attraction" stuff in a lot of professional and spiritual settings, and it does nothing to help you change your situation – it just piles on a bunch of judgment and guilt on top of what you're already experiencing.

Most women who have experienced harassment know this kind of blame all too well. We are assumed to be honest until we challenge a man in authority, and then our believability comes into question – suddenly it is like we are dirty and there is something wrong with us that created this other person's bad behavior. People start telling us that they "believe" us as though that is a gift and the default were to assume we're liars. This adds so much judgment on top of the fear you are already experiencing.

Jennifer Freyd, a professor at the University of Oregon, does research on the concept of "institutional betrayal," which she defines as "wrongdoings perpetrated by an institution upon individuals dependent on that institution, including failure to prevent or respond supportively to wrongdoings by individuals (e.g. sexual assault) committed within the context of the institution." For many of us, harassment itself is an experience of institutional betrayal if we experience it in a place we think is supposed to be safe. For example, when a man brags about his feminism and progressive politics and then turns around and harasses women, the hypocrisy can become a betrayal. Then, when we start to talk about the harassment, we often experience another level of betrayal when institutions and support people are not willing to become allies.

This can be genuinely devastating, and so nothing I am saying in here is meant to minimize that. I am saying all of this with the purpose of empowering you. Trying to spread some kind of positive, wishful thinking on top of that betrayal only makes us feel worse.

Managing your thinking is the key to that empowerment, though, and not in a fake way of forcing yourself to think things you don't really believe are true. When I strategize with my clients, I help them map out their plan for the actions they want to take and the results they want to get. All of that starts with their thinking. If the only result you get from changing your thinking is to truly take back your power over your time and energy, that would be enough. But, what I often see, when my clients truly start to use this strategy to defend their careers and claim the work they love as their own, is that they are also able to make institutional and social change as well.

Your Thoughts Create Your Feelings

Most of us want to feel good all the time. That makes sense – it sucks to feel fear, loneliness, shame, or grief. But, we run into problems because almost no one wants to feel good about harassment. Almost no one wants to feel good about death. Harassment and death exist, so sometimes we *want* to feel crappy.

The people who want to feel good about those things are sociopaths. So, if you are being harassed and you feel terrible most of the time, the good news is that you are human. You probably *want* to feel terrible about harassment.

We get stuck, though, when we think that the harassment is in control of our feelings.

Your thoughts create your feelings. Nothing in the outside world creates your feelings. You can know this is true because if someone you love is living in another state and dies, you do not feel grief at the exact moment of the death. You feel grief when you learn about the death and think a thought about it.

As we discussed before, most of the approximately 60,000 thoughts we have each day happen on the unconscious level. That is why it seems like our feelings come from the circumstances of the outside world. Most of our thoughts are so patterned and unconscious that we do not even notice them.

But, the world is as sharp as a knife. The Buddhist monk Shantideva says, "Where would there be leather enough to cover the entire world? With just the leather of my sandals, it is as if the whole world were covered. Likewise, I am unable to restrain external phenomena, but I shall restrain my own mind."

What he means in our context is that harassment is not going to go away, at least not overnight, but possibly not ever. Violence is not going to go away. Discrimination is not going to go away. To use the hand washing analogy, people understand now that hand washing saves lives, but we still fail to do it and spread germs. Germs are not going away. Similarly, it is unlikely that discrimination will just disappear in our lifetime. This life is supposed to be sharp.

But, that does not mean you need to feel terrible. Managing your thinking is like putting shoes on to walk out into the world instead of trying to cover the world in padding. You can try to pad the world, but you will probably end up trapped at home because there is not enough padding to make the world soft.

Usually, what I see with my clients is that they think that their harasser has to change what he is doing in order for them to feel better. But, this is almost always demonstrably not true. For example, I had a client whose boss would come up behind her quietly and put his hand on her shoulder. She experienced shame, terror, and overwhelm just in that second of him putting his hand on her shoulder. But, she also had a teenage son. I asked her if she would feel shame, terror, and overwhelm if her teenage son put his hand on her shoulder, and the answer was obviously, no. She chose to think that her boss putting his hand on her shoulder was a power play that meant she was trapped and did not deserve respect. With her son, though, she chose to think he might not understand that she didn't want him up in her business. She told me she was frozen in fear with her boss, but she would easily tell her son not to touch her.

Those two different thoughts create very different feelings, but the action initiating them is the same. And I hear you if you want to say that a boss touching her is very different than her own child touching her. The point, though, is not *his* behavior. The point is that *she* had power over what she was thinking about the behavior. And those thoughts created her feeling, not the outside circumstance of someone touching her shoulder.

Your Feelings Motivate Your Actions

I remember in law school, I was in my first-year criminal law class, and this very loud, blustery, fragile man raised his hand to complain about something, probably study materials for our final. I was telling someone about it later, and I said something like, "Zach doesn't like the study materials because they hurt his feelings." What can I say? It's fun to be a jerk sometimes. I love consulting with lawyers about developing a career defense plan because they are *so uncomfortable* when I tell them that part of it is identifying feelings. Lawyers hate feelings. It's hilarious.

Most professionals hate feelings, though. Now that I think about it, maybe most humans hate identifying feelings. Most of us choose numbness rather than the wild rebellion of our bodies when a feeling passes through.

So, if you are in that camp, you are not alone.

Here's why it's important to practice identifying feelings: Your feelings motivate what you do or don't do. If we feel sad, we do nothing. If we feel motivated, we get things done. You don't get to feel motivated all of the time because life includes both positive and negative, and our brains are drawn more towards negative (remember that identifying the negative kept our ancestors alive) than positive.

If you think you can do the hard work to overcome harassment in your life without experiencing your feelings, good luck, but I have not seen a way.

There is no feeling that is wrong or bad. Some are painful and some are comforting, but resisting any of them creates all kinds of stuckness, drama, and chaos.

Right now, your thoughts are already creating your feelings, and your feelings are motivating what you do or don't do. You are already in control of your feelings, even if it does not seem that way. If you need to make a change in what you are doing in order to have your best possible reaction to harassment, that starts with shifting your thinking.

We learn to allow feelings to have space by literally just sitting and purposely choosing the feeling. So, for example, if you are feeling anxious when you think about going back to your work, it is likely that on some level you may be resisting how you feel. Resistance looks like, "Oh my god, get over it! You're fine! Stop even thinking about it! No one else has a problem but you." Allowing the feeling looks like, "What if it made sense for me to choose this anxiety? What would it look like to choose this anxiety on purpose?"

We usually don't want to choose negative feelings because we are convinced that they will last forever and we'll get sucked into a spiral if we choose them. But, if we can choose them with compassion, and really understand they are just a sensation in your body (less painful than a broken leg, usually), they really do not last forever (or even as long as a broken leg). It is actually when we resist the feelings that they tend to last, and then we get stuck in doing nothing. We get into that negotiation with them, where we are both trying to shut them down and trying to prove they are our only option. Allowing that they are one reasonable way to feel lets us move on to consider our other options.

In the example above, when my client would feel shame, terror, and overwhelm after her boss touched her shoulder, those feelings would motivate her to freeze and argue with herself about what she did to cause his behavior. When her son would touch her shoulder, she might feel annoyed and capable, and those feelings would motivate her to tell him to stop.

When we have a repeating pattern of holding ourselves back and trying to ignore harassment, it can feel like there are no other options. There are always other options.

Your Actions Create Your Results

If you want to make real change in your personal experience, and (I hope) real institutional change through your experience, you will need to take huge action. As Tony Robbins calls it, "massive action." Responding to harassment is not for the weak. It is for true warriors who are willing to fight for justice, not just for themselves, but for our mothers who suffered the same or worse, for our friends who know what we are going through, and for the little girls who will come after us.

The good news is that taking massive action does not mean your harasser has to change or that you have to pad the world so that it is comfortable for you. But it does mean creating the exact life you want. Sound daunting? It is hard work, but it is so worth it. You creating the exact life you want is rebellion against harassment, and it creates its own institutional change.

If what you want is to be successful in your profession based on your hard work and dedication, while your harasser has to back down and get out of your life, that is absolutely a result you can create by managing your thinking. Managing your thinking creates the feelings that will motivate the massive action to create the results you want. Taking massive action means continuing to take action, despite failures and discomfort, until you get the results you want.

Trying to ignore harassment makes space for harassment and often rewards it. The actions my clients usually decide to take are to talk, take up space, set consequences, create success in a specific way to them, and be willing to fail. Those actions move my clients forward and crush the harassment around them. They create the results that my clients want, no matter how other people behave. You may think you are not capable of that, but everyone is capable of that. Your thought that you can't do it is the only thing holding you back.

How to Manage Your Thinking

There are many supports for managing your thinking. Meditation is one – just sitting and drawing your thought back to one neutral thing (for example, your breathing) helps refocus your thoughts. Byron Katie's

"The Work" is another simple tool that I often use with clients to manage their thinking. Most thought work fits well with legal issues because it all questions the truth of our thinking and what our evidence is.

The tool I use most often, though, is Brooke Castillo's self-coaching thought model. It goes like this:

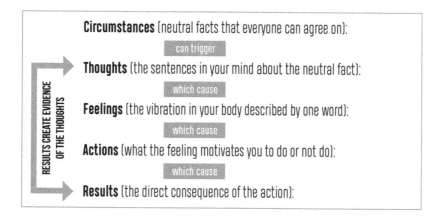

When we are coaching, I write out my clients' thought models like this:

C:
T:
F:
A:
R:

One of the most common thought models I encounter with my clients, and one I work on myself as well, is this:

C: A man said words
T: There is something wrong with me and I deserve disrespect.
F: Shame

A: Hide

R: He gets what he wants and I don't stand up for myself.

When you look at the model as I've written it, it seems clear that the neutral fact, "A man said words" is not creating the thought, "There is something wrong with me and I deserve disrespect."

But, what if the man was old and gross and said, "You must not have been listening," or "You're so cute," or "That's not what I asked for, you need to pay attention," or "I bet your boyfriend is happy at night," or any of the other sleazeball things men sometimes say? Would that cause the feeling of shame?

Most clients say at this point, "No no no, you don't understand *what* he said to me." I do understand. I get that he is gross without even hearing what he said because I trust you. Now it's time to take your power back.

No sleazeball man can cause your feeling of shame. It is always your thought that creates your feeling. For example, if a sleazeball man said to you, "I hate that you have two heads," you would probably not feel shame because you would not agree that you have two heads. You would probably not choose the thought "There's something wrong with me and I deserve disrespect." You might think something more like, "That's weird, and he may need a mental health consultation," which would create a feeling like wariness or curiosity.

The key to changing our thinking patterns is in what we make our harasser's behavior mean about us. Remember, there is nothing you are doing to cause your harasser's behavior. He is responsible for his behavior. You are responsible for yourself and your feelings. His behavior is basically none of your business, except for how you want to take care of yourself and protect yourself around it.

That is great news because you can feel good and create the exact life you want without it being tied to his behavior. If he is harassing you, he is the *last* person you want to have control over how you feel or what you do.

The change we make in changing our story and what we make harassment mean about us is not to go from fear and shame directly to sunshine and rainbows. None of this is about convincing yourself of lies or being fake. This is about recognizing the ways that you are siding with your harasser and giving him the power that is inherently yours.

Sometimes we want to give away our power because it feels easier for other people to take care of us and manage our feelings than doing it ourselves. But, it is actually way, *way* harder. If you want your harasser to be managing your thoughts and feelings, you have to manage his behavior or feel terrible all the time. His behavior is really difficult to manage, especially if you are trying to avoid it.

In order to take back your power and manage your own thoughts and feelings, one step is to try on a neutral thought. (This is similar to how, with meditation, we come back, over and over again, when our minds wander, to something neutral like breath.) A neutral thought is something everyone can agree on. For example, if you have practiced the thought, "There is something wrong with me," it probably won't be believable to force the thought "I'm perfect just the way I am," and that's okay. Trying to force or fake a positive thought just reinforces the negative thought because your brain knows when you're being fake. Instead, try on the thought, "I am a human." That thought should be believable and give you some relief from the shame of "There's something wrong with me." Then, be curious about moving towards a belief like, "I am human and it's possible that humans deserve respect." If that feels false to you, practice the thought "I am human."

I call this process mapping a new belief.

NEGATIVE	NEUTRAL	POSSIBLE	POSITIVE
"There is something wrong with me."	"I am a human"	"It's possible there are good things about me."	"I'm perfect the way I am."

When we first start recognizing that our thinking is creating our results, it is easy to become very judgmental about our negative thoughts. They are not creating the results we want, they feel terrible, and yet we keep choosing them. That kind of judgment just brings us back to a struggle with ourselves instead of letting us move forward to create the change we want. There is nothing *wrong* with your negative beliefs, but they are a choice. If you wanted to actively continue to believe a painful thought, I might disagree with you about it, but it would still be your choice.

A negative belief is "negative" because it moves us backwards or keeps us motionless, not because it is "evil" or "stupid." A "positive" belief is "positive" because it moves us forward. Negative beliefs also tend to be painful, but sometimes we want to feel painful feelings. Again, I don't want to feel chipper about harassment. But, I do want to feel the power of knowing that my anger over harassment is my choice.

The purpose of this is not to eliminate the thought "There is something wrong with me," or to start judging yourself about having chosen a thought like that. The purpose is to recognize it is a choice to think that thought, and there are tons of other thoughts that are believable options. They are neither right nor wrong, and many of them, positive or negative, are reasonable. But, each creates a feeling, which creates an action, and when we are not deliberate about our thoughts, but let our unconscious take over, we often create patterns of helplessness.

When we are stuck in a pattern of helplessness, we are not going to change our results. You can yell at yourself all you want, but you are unlikely to beat yourself into defending your career from harassment. When you are harassing yourself with your own thinking, it is almost impossible to take a stance against a harasser who is not in your head. The easiest, most efficient way to change our results starts with our thinking.

What Do You Want to Create?

The next question is what you want to create in the world and in your experience of harassment. Do you want to let your brain align with your harasser's views or think thoughts that are probably even crueler than his? I'm guessing you don't. So, the next step is to reverse engineer the thought model in a way that starts with what you want. For example:

C: A man said words
T:
F:
A:
R: Stop the harassment

What do you need to do in order to get that result? (put that in the A line)

How do you need to feel in order to take that action? (put that in the F line)

What thought creates that feeling? (put that in the T line)

That thought is going to be the key to getting the result you want. But, if it does not seem believable to you or you can't come up with a thought that creates the feeling you want, you are completely normal.

This is very high-level thought management work, so don't give up if you are confused. I have a coach, my coach has a coach, her coach has a coach, and so forth. We are not meant to do this work on our own, and if you would like more help, it is here for you.

Often the feeling we want to create that will drive the actions we want is "confidence." But, we believe we can't feel confident until we find proof we are capable. That creates a whole trap where we can't ever move forward because we can find so much evidence that undermines our confidence.

Instead, here is the thought model I would suggest to get you started if this thought feels believable:

C: A man said words.
T: I am committed to taking care of myself – no matter what.
F: Committed
A: Take care of myself no matter what.
R: Stop the harassment

Or what about this?

C: A man said words.
T: I am brave enough to take care of myself, even if it is uncomfortable and I make mistakes.
F: Courage
A: Take care of myself.
R: Stop the harassment.

If those do not feel believable, you can always go back to "I am human and it's possible humans deserve respect."

───────────── ACTION STEPS: ─────────────

Email me at Meredith@FreedomResourceCenter.com to get a copy of the Personal Career Defense Toolkit. Include "Toolkit" in the subject line of your email. Or, find your own notebook or blank sheet of paper to fill out these steps.

Make sure that wherever you write this, it includes a notice that what you write is in anticipation of talking with an attorney and pursuing a legal claim. That means it should be attorney-client or work-product privileged. Talk with an attorney in your state to get the details of what that means.

1. Write down all of the thoughts you have about your harasser. Don't edit, just write them as they come.
2. What do you make that mean about yourself?
3. Pick one thought you've written down and fill in a thought model.

C: (The neutral fact that everyone, including your harasser, could agree on.)
T: (The sentence in your mind about the neutral circumstance.)
F: (The one-word vibration in your body created by the thought.)
A: (What the feeling motivates you to do or not do.)
R: (The direct consequence of the action.)

1. Write a conscious model, using the reverse-engineering method above. This is what you want to create.
2. Use the mapping tool above to create a path from your negative belief to a positive belief. Include a neutral belief and a possible belief that you can practice in order to transition from the negative to the positive.

Chapter 6

Strategy 4: Action

When I was in high school, I was part of a mega church in the tiny town of Applegate, Oregon. It actually wasn't even in Applegate – that's a lie – it was in an even tinier town 10 miles down the road called Ruch that was basically only the church. At one point, they had a ministry training program at the church that only men were allowed to attend because women weren't allowed to lead in the church. All of the hottest 20-something guys in the church went into the ministry training, and it soon turned into a marriage factory. One year, I went to 18 weddings. I learned to completely loathe weddings and showers of every kind.

But, I still always said "yes" when I was invited to one. I didn't want to hurt people's feelings; I wanted to be nice. I had all kinds of excuses.

Now, I pride myself on my honesty and integrity, and I have always felt like my integrity was a core part of who I am. But, you know what a people-pleaser actually is? A liar. I had to realize that if I am lying about what I want in order to keep other people from feeling negative feelings, I am outside of my integrity, manipulating them. When I was saying "yes" to things I did not want to do, I did it because I had developed a justification in my head that my lying about what I wanted was a noble sacrifice for other people. Somehow, I thought that lying was helping the people I was manipulating, instead of just protecting myself from discomfort.

On the other hand, when I went to law school, I wanted it. Like, I *wanted* it. I wanted all the late nights and anxiety and demeaning professors. I wanted the whole experience. When my friends would complain about how they hated law school and were making some kind of sacrifice by being there, I was not impressed. "Just leave," I would always think. It seemed disrespectful to a challenge I embraced that they would talk about it like it was a sacrifice.

But, I have realized that my "noble sacrifice" of going to someone's baby shower is exactly the same as my friends complaining about law school when they had the privilege to be there. I have come to realize that my friends having showers *might actually want to have a shower*. Shocking, I know. But, it might be true. I have sometimes heard people say, "That game at your shower was so fun!" I know you're as shocked as I am, but part of growing up is letting people be different than us. Scientists should be researching this issue if they are not already. I can see the study title as I write, "Baby Shower: Cruel Torture Chamber or Thing Someone Might Actually Want to Have? A Qualitative Research Study."

Greg McKeown, in the book *Essentialism*, says, "The reality is, saying yes to any opportunity by definition requires saying no to several others."

Read that quote again because it's so important.

Every time I lie by saying "yes" to something I don't want, I am also lying in saying "no" to what I do want. Wow! Don't pretend this is old news. Still, every time I read that sentence, my brain feels like it's bending.

Read it again.

Wow.

When you say yes to something, it is a big deal. I would even say, if I were in a poetical mood, it is a sacred gift. Your "yes" is important. Taking action to defend your career against sexual harassment and to advance in fulfilling work means practicing saying "yes" to yourself.

As women, we are often taught that it is our responsibility to manage relationships and that managing relationships requires us to read and manage other people's feelings. When we say "no" to someone, we expect them to have negative feelings about it. Then, we think those negative feelings are our fault and we did something wrong to create those negative feelings in the other person.

I can lie and say "yes," that I "want to go" to my friend's baby shower because I think she'll be happy I'm coming, and it's "not that big of a deal." Then, I can take credit for her happiness and think I've done something noble to create it.

Yuck!

Living my life like that means that I'm surrounding myself with people who will be happy at my unhappiness. And, it turns me into the victim of my friends' happiness. Also, here's the other thing: if I let go of some of the pressure I'm putting on myself for "having" to say "yes" to certain things, sometimes I discover that I actually *want* to say yes, even to a baby shower. Not very often on that one. If you're having a baby, remind me to send a gift.

"How does this nonsense apply to ending harassment?" I hear you ask.

There is a great deal of focus in the law and in society on whether or not we should put pressure on women to say "no" when they are confronted with harassing behavior. This is an issue that can get overly complicated because it makes no sense to say a woman is at fault for doing nothing, and on the other hand say that the man is not responsible for outrageous behavior. (Even though that is basically how we handle harassment situations all the time, it still makes no sense.)

In reality, it basically comes down to what I have said before: You are never responsible for your harasser's bad behavior, but you are responsible for your own feelings. When we are compromising our "yesses," it feels crappy. This is not because it's your job to stop men from harassing people. It's because if you are already experiencing terrible behavior from some man, you don't want to be on his side, also harassing yourself. If you are holding yourself back from what you truly want or indulging in confusion about moving forward and taking up space in your life, that is like being on your harasser's side.

When we are taking responsibility for other people's anger or disappointment, and contorting our lives to make sure no one around us ever feels bad, we end up feeling gross all the time. We become a second harasser to ourselves.

You don't have a duty to anyone else to say "yes" or "no," but you have a responsibility to take care of yourself and your feelings. Honoring your yesses and taking massive action to get what you want, even if someone else has a negative reaction to it, requires courage and strengthens your muscle of self-respect. It also respects the other person enough to let them choose the thoughts and feelings that are best for them. When I go to my friend's baby shower out of sacrifice, thinking that she can't deal with the negative feelings of not having me there, it's pretty arrogant. People are going to have to handle their own negative feelings, no matter what you do.

Also, people are supposed to feel bad sometimes. You choosing to feel gross and stressed out because you are compromising your "yesses" does not help anyone else. The even crazier news is that it probably does not even change what the other person is feeling at all. Most of the time, our feelings are related to judgments we have about ourselves more than they are related to our thoughts about anyone else.

"Just because someone else is a jerk doesn't mean I want to be a jerk," I hear you say. Fair. I don't want you to be a jerk either.

Being deliberate about where you put your "yesses" and honoring those decisions is not being a jerk. Remember, you are *already* saying no to multiple things every time you say yes to, or go along with, something you don't want to do.

Passing on offers in order to put our time into what we truly want is often difficult both because we want to make other people happy and because we have FOMO (Fear of Missing Out). Both of these are usually based in mind-reading negative thoughts into other people's heads and fortune telling worst-case-scenarios. Because our brains work so hard to invent negative consequences, we lose sight of what we want to create and get wrapped up in trying to protect against a disastrous future scenario. Master Coach Kara Loewentheil said it this way: "If someone asked you to go murder kittens with them, would you say yes to make them happy or because you were afraid of missing out?" That was a clear, easy, no for me. Sacrificing what you were meant to create by compromising your "yesses" is sacrificing a human life (yours). That is not nobler than murdering kittens.

When you are deliberate about saying yes, it puts you in an active, leadership role in your own life. It doesn't mean you will say "no" more than you already do, but it may change how you say no. For example, McKeown, in *Essentialism*, also explains that we almost never actually have to say no. Instead, we can say things like, "It is great to hear from you. Thanks so much for thinking of me, but for several reasons I can't commit to that." You can always be polite in your "no-thank-you," and still choose the "yes" that is right for you.

At every step in your life you are saying "yes" to one thing and "no" to many others. Saying "no" to yourself is not nobler than saying "no" to someone else.

My other favorite "yes" person is Marie Kondo. (Sorry, Shondra Rhimes. You seem nice too.) A few years ago, I tidied my home using her *Life Changing Magic of Tidying Up* book, and it completely refocused my brain to see what I was rejecting in my life, just by default of saying "yes" to things I didn't like. For example, in my shirt drawer, I found a whole stack of shirts I loved underneath a pile of shirts I was keeping because it seemed wasteful to get rid of them.

As Kondo explains in her book, the process about being deliberate about what we say yes to in our possessions is analogous to what we say yes to in our personal and professional lives. If I say yes to junk in my home, it is likely I am saying yes to junk in my professional life (and vice versa). If I am saying no to things I love in my home by piling things I don't like on top of them, I am likely doing the same in my professional life.

With whom do you have lunch out of obligation?

Whom do you text back when you don't want to talk?

When do you say yes to other people and, by default, say no to yourself?

Being "self-sacrificing" is really different than being compassionate. Pema Chodron explains, "Compassion is not a relationship between the healer and the wounded. It's a relationship between equals. Only when we know our own darkness well can we be present with the darkness of others. Compassion becomes real when we recognize our shared humanity."

Self-sacrifice, in itself, really has nothing to do with anyone but yourself. There is no rule that says you have to be uncomfortable in order for other people to have comfort. Rather, this type of thinking sets us up against other people, even people we love. It says, in order for you to be happy, I must be in pain.

I don't want people to be in pain for me. Other people's pain doesn't benefit me.

I'm not going to tell you that discomfort is worthless. In fact, I think discomfort is incredibly valuable. But, there is a big difference between self-indulgent, manipulative discomfort and the discomfort of challenge and integrity. When we are indulging in our own discomfort and blaming it on other people, we become a victim. When we expect other people to be uncomfortable so that we can be happy, we become a vampire. Bad news either way.

When we choose to say "yes" to challenging discomfort and to standing in the integrity of who we are and what we want, we grow. Sometimes this is painful to the people around us who can't keep up with our growth, or the people who want to bleed us dry because we always say yes to them, even when we don't mean it. But, it is still more honest to those people.

Part of defending your career from sexual harassment is becoming curious about what you are saying "yes" to. I remember, early in my career, when my boss would touch me every time he saw me, giving me huge shoulder rubs, rubbing down my arms, and leaning his entire body against me. I was not saying yes to that, and every time it happened, I would be shocked at myself that I didn't push him off or react in some way to protect myself. It wasn't like me.

Saying "yes" to myself in that situation, protecting my body, did not start with me pushing a man, in a much higher power position than me, off of my body and telling him never to touch me again. It started with a much smaller "yes." It started with saying yes to telling my friends and people I trusted about what was happening. It started with saying "yes" to a colleague who asked me if my boss ever made me uncomfortable. It started with small "yesses" that honored my experience and my story. Once I was able to honor those steps, I could move to what seemed like an impossible yes of listening to my body's warning signals and respecting them when anyone touched me without my permission. It requires checking in with your core about small steps and choices.

In general, if we are going to make big changes like this and take big action, it is important to choose a very compelling reason to do it. My compelling reason was that I knew if I kept living in fear I would die.

I knew that my clients needed my help and my example. I knew that I wanted to say yes to my clients and myself, but I was giving all my yesses to my harasser. I had to make a shift. There was no other choice.

If we don't choose a compelling reason to honor what we want, we often stay stuck in confusion and believe it is too hard to figure out what we want. Then, it gives us an excuse to look outside of ourselves for the answer. That is another form of indulgence and naturally leads to people pleasing (manipulating other people). What if the words "I don't know" did not exist? You would have to start building a relationship with the integrity of who you are at your core and what you want, even in small choices. You would have to start checking in with yourself, instead of the people around you, about your next steps. Having that relationship of integrity with yourself can be uncomfortable, but it is the discomfort of action.

───────────── ACTION STEPS: ─────────────

Email me at Meredith@FreedomResourceCenter.com to get a copy of the Personal Career Defense Toolkit. Include "Toolkit" in the subject line of your email. Or, find your own notebook or blank sheet of paper to fill out these steps.

Make sure that wherever you write this, it includes a notice that what you write is in anticipation of talking with an attorney and pursuing a legal claim. That means it should be attorney-client or work-product privileged. Talk with an attorney in your state to get the details of what that means.

1. What do you say yes to now that creates a healthy relationship with your body?
2. What do you say yes to now that creates healthy relationships with other people?
3. What do you say yes to now, when you really mean no?

4. What would you say yes to in your wildest dreams, if nothing were impossible?
5. What is a compelling reason to make a change?

Chapter 7

Strategy 5: Consequences

I was consulting with a lawyer whose supervising attorney was being a tyrant to her because she was a woman. It was one of those situations where you just know he would not have talked to a man the way he was talking to her, but he wasn't outright calling her "baby doll" or anything like that. Instead, he was questioning every answer she gave him, criticizing her for lacking confidence, and saying behind her back that he wasn't sure why but she just wasn't ready for major responsibility.

We talked one day when she was particularly upset and she was thinking about quitting her job. She said she didn't need to continue to take someone undermining her at every turn.

(As I'm telling you this story, I realize that I'm actually mixing up three different stories with different clients because I have been having this conversation so often recently.)

What she said was completely true. She did not need to continue to tolerate anything she didn't like. But, the issue I take with this thinking, as my clients' advocate, is that quitting almost always punishes the woman experiencing the harassment and rewards the man doing the harassing. I understand that my client's supervising attorney had invested money in her by hiring her, but losing that investment is not nearly as impactful to him as her losing her source of income.

Quitting makes it much, much more difficult to bring a legal claim for harassment because the law expects us to do the heavy lifting of ending discrimination, and it only steps in when that's not possible. There are different standards for a legal claim if a woman quits because of harassment than if she gets fired.

Quitting says, "Okay, you own this mountain, so I'll back down and go find a different mountain." It gives ground and space to someone as a reward for their bad behavior. Usually, it is us giving up space and letting a man take that space over. Defending our careers from sexual harassment means standing in our space and claiming it for ourselves, despite someone else having bad behavior. It is not easy, but it is worth it.

Don't get me wrong, if you are in physical danger, call 911, leave, and do whatever you need to do to keep yourself safe. It is much more common with my clients, though, that they want their jobs, they are excellent at their jobs, and they are not in physical danger.

Their brains, though, are telling them that they are about to be eaten by a tiger. Our brains, as we discussed before, have not yet evolved to know the difference between our supervising attorney, or our business competitor, our CEO, or some guy on the internet throwing a tantrum and a giant tiger attack. This just means that you have to process your brain's immediate reaction that you're going to die before you can make a deliberate decision about what the consequence will be for tantrum behavior next time.

And there will be a next time. If you are working with a giant toddler today, he will still be a giant toddler tomorrow. Physics exists. Often, part of a harassing or abusive experience is that the harasser seems to change day-to-day, and some days he will be really encouraging and nice. Then, it feels like the rug is pulled out from under you on the day he returns to throwing tantrums.

Here's the thing: I am a jerk sometimes. I am not a particularly thoughtful person, and my best friend describes that I don't mean to say arrogant things, I'm just an Aries and it's my nature. She's totally right, and also, I think sometimes it's hilarious when I'm sarcastic or contrary. I like that about me. Tomorrow, I might listen to a podcast that really hits me about being a better listener and self-reflect about how I want to build more connection and really understand the people around me without attachment to outcome. So, tomorrow, I might ask particularly thoughtful questions and really take to heart what people say to me.

I am still going to go back to being sarcastic and contrary because I think it's hilarious. But, I am not going to punch you in the face. Honestly, I'm probably not going to punch you in the face even if I'm in physical danger because it just freaks me out.

Sarcastic and contrary is on the acceptable side of the line for me, punching you in the face is on the unacceptable side of the line.

People do not change their understanding of what falls on the acceptable and unacceptable sides of the line overnight. In order to change that, people have to practice change and have a compelling reason to practice change. Like with making your own change from saying yes to your harasser to saying yes to yourself and the people you love, it takes a compelling reason for your harasser to change. Your discomfort may not even register on his radar, and it probably is not compelling enough to him to motivate his change. Until you or someone else creates a compelling reason for him to change, your harasser may say one day that he completely understands his behavior was unacceptable, and then turn around and do the same thing again a month later.

This is normal and expected. He is going to still be him tomorrow and the next day. Making more space for his harassment gives him a compelling reason to keep harassing.

It is not your job to change him, even if he has kids and you're worried about how his behavior will affect his kids. Your job is to take care of yourself, protect yourself, and create the exact, ideal life you want. You standing your ground and setting consequences may also help his kids, but getting into their business about it will only distract you from setting consequences. Harassment will still exist even if you become perfect at defending your career against it, but if it comes into your space, there are consequences.

I was consulting with a woman who works for a major investment banking company in a department made up almost exclusively of men. She had multiple inappropriate experiences at work, but she was also struggling with dating because of more than one experience where a man had physically intimidated or hurt her. She described her insight saying, "What if I just always expect that if I am on a date with a man I don't know, he could try to force me to do something I don't want to do, and then I just plan ahead of time how I will respond to take care of myself?" She realized that part of what would happen in these situations for her was that she was so shocked in the moment that someone would be that inappropriate that she had a delayed response in protecting herself. She had trained in mixed martial arts and jujitsu, and so her ability to take care of herself was not a problem. Her problem was that she did not have a plan ahead of time, so it took her time to even acknowledge the inappropriate behavior.

Again, that is not to say at all that she was responsible for the behavior of the men. Yes, parents should train boys to be respectful more than they train girls to avoid walking at night. But, we already have generations of men who were not trained that way, and they need consequences as much as we need protection.

You already know the behavior that your harasser is willing to engage in. You know the line he is willing to cross. Assume he is going to keep being him. Lundy Bancroft goes into this idea in more detail in *Why Does He Do That?*, describing that people often blame alcohol, drugs, or mental illness for abusive behavior in men. Really, he explains, there are alcoholics, drug addicts, and mentally ill men who are not willing to hit people or engage in other cruelty. So, the line a person draws is not caused by substances or mental illness. A person chooses where that line is, and then substances or mental illness may make that behavior more extreme on the side of the line the person finds acceptable.

Bancroft runs a program for men convicted of violence against women. One example Bancroft gives of his argument that abusers have a line they draw, whether or not substances or mental illness is involved, relates to the men in his program who describe that they "lost control" and started hitting someone. Bancroft asks them, "Why didn't you kill her?" And the men respond, "Oh, I would never do that!" But, if they truly "lost control," there is nothing they would be able to do to prevent themselves from murder.

Because the behavior we are talking about often seems so charged, sometimes I explain it this way. Imagine, you come across a bunny rabbit, and you really want it to stop hopping and walk on its hind legs like a person. You think it's outrageous for anything to do so much hopping, when for you walking is very natural and much more dignified. So, you do everything you can think of to get the rabbit to stop hopping. You say "yes" to everything it asks of you; you respond to its every call morning and night; you sometimes get angry and yell at it or cry and demand an explanation; you do everything you can to change your behavior to get it to stop hopping. Still, the bunny rabbit hops.

The point I want to get across is obviously not that harassment is like a bunny rabbit hopping, but that someone's harassing behavior belongs to that person and is about him, not about you. If he is willing to do it, especially if he is willing to do it more than once, that means it is as natural, normal, and acceptable to him as hopping is to a bunny rabbit. You changing your behavior, sacrificing anything about yourself, making yourself smaller, or being unhappy is not going to change that because it is about him, not about you.

The truth is that people are in control of themselves when they are harassing or abusive. There are lines they are willing to cross, and lines they will not cross. Especially when they face no real consequences for their behavior (sometimes even when they do face consequences for their behavior), they don't see any reason to change. When we make ourselves smaller in response to harassment, it rewards the bad behavior.

When Leaving is the Right Answer

Leaving is the right answer when it is the best answer for you to take you to the next level of who you were meant to become. Don't leave until you are leaving from a place of power and love. The one exception I would give is that, if you are in immediate physical danger, always leave if you can and call 911. If you are not in immediate physical danger, going through this is what will strengthen you and show you what is possible for you.

Staying and standing your ground in any kind of harassing situation does not mean sitting back and taking it or ignoring it. It means clearly identifying where your boundaries are and enforcing them with consequences. Staying is for *you*, and it does not mean giving up any of your space.

Setting a personal boundary is like setting a property boundary. If your neighbor starts coming through your door, you would probably (I hope) tell him to leave or you'll call the police. The same is true with setting your personal boundaries. In order for you to need to enforce a boundary, there needs to first be a boundary violation. This is different than being deliberate about what *you* say "yes" to. So, for example, if your business partner does not appreciate your work or pull his weight in the office, that is not a boundary violation. You always, in that situation, have the opportunity to say yes or no to picking up the extra weight and to choose how you want to feel about his level of appreciation. That has nothing to do with boundaries.

If your business partner is coming into your office without knocking or yelling at you in public, that may be a boundary violation. You get to decide if that behavior crosses your boundaries and what the consequences will be (to take care of yourself) if it does.

When we want someone to do something so that we can feel better (appreciated, happy, safe, satisfied, or any other good feeling), that is like having an instruction manual for how they will act to make us feel good. That kind of situation is like what we talked about in Chapter 6 with me and my baby shower struggle. A friend may want me to come to her baby shower, but it does not violate her boundaries for me to say no to that invitation. She can choose to be unhappy or angry about that, but it still would not be because I crossed a boundary.

On the other hand, if I showed up in the middle of the night at her house, that may be a boundary violation.

You don't have to tolerate any behavior you don't like, but setting consequences is different than trying to control or manipulate people to make ourselves feel better. For example, I had a friend living with me to get away from a violent boyfriend. I knew that if she was not honest with me about continuing to talk to him or if he came over to the house, she could not continue to live with me. When that happened, we found another place for her to live. It was not because I was angry with her, and I absolutely still loved her, but it was just the consequence I needed to set to make sure I was safe.

One common consequence I recommend for inappropriate sexual comments or touching in a professional setting is talking about the behavior and reporting it. Just talking about someone else's bad behavior protects you from taking responsibility for it. If you talk about it, make sure you are talking about it in a way that makes it clear it is not your responsibility and that takes care of you around the behavior. Remember, the purpose of setting a consequence is to protect yourself, not to punish the other person. Other consequences are just walking away, locking a door, changing the locks on doors, calling the police, or documenting behavior in writing and emailing it to multiple people including the harasser.

If you are doing any of these behaviors as revenge, that is really different than setting consequences for a boundary violation. Consequences are always to protect you, which is your business. How he feels about something is none of your business – not because wanting revenge means something about you, but because it feels terrible *for* you. If you get wrapped up in how he feels, whether you want him to feel bad or good, that is a big win for him. It means you are taking care of him (even if you are punishing him) rather than taking care of yourself. That's two people on his side, and zero on yours.

Be your own advocate. Defend *your* career, don't attack his – he is already on a self-destruct path, and you don't need to get caught in its wake. Be on your own side. I'm already on your side, and I know you can do it.

─────────── ACTION STEPS ───────────

Email me at Meredith@FreedomResourceCenter.com to get a copy of the Personal Career Defense Toolkit. Include "Toolkit" in the subject line of your email. Or, find your own notebook or blank sheet of paper to fill out these steps.

Make sure that wherever you write this, it includes a notice that what you write is in anticipation of talking with an attorney and pursuing a legal claim. That means it should be attorney-client or work-product privileged. Talk with an attorney in your state to get the details of what that means.

1. Who is behaving in a way you don't like?
2. How do you want the behavior to change?
3. How would you feel if the behavior changed?

4. What would you be thinking about yourself if the behavior changed?
5. What are you thinking about yourself now?
6. What is a boundary violation you are experiencing?
7. What is a consequence you want to set for that boundary violation?

Chapter 8

—— ✲ ——

Strategy 6: Creation

"If someone comes along and shoots an arrow into your heart, it's fruitless to stand there and yell at the person. It would be much better to turn your attention to the fact that there's an arrow in your heart."

— PEMA CHODRON, Start Where You Are

Honestly, when I ask my clients what they want out of bringing a claim for sexual harassment, while there are a lot of common responses ("I don't want this to happen to anyone else," "I want my life back," etc.) one of the most common responses is "I want him to be accountable for what he did" or "I want him to pay." Judge all you want about the dangers of getting obsessed with revenge, and we all know there are dangers, but it is totally normal to want an entitled jerk who tortured you to pay for what he did.

When I said in the last chapter that doing things out of revenge is a bad idea because it gets you taking care of his feelings instead of yours, I wasn't making that up. But, you have to start moving forward from a realistic idea of where you are. If you want revenge, the key is to make sure that the desire for revenge channels to something productive for you and doesn't just give your harasser power over you for the rest of your life. He is the last person you want to have power over your future.

The best revenge is creating the exact life you want. The best career defense is a good career offense. It may not seem like that totally crushes your harasser into the muck and slime of his own despicableness, but it does. The more you create, the more you rise up, the more he is buried under your success.

This kind of thinking does not have the (sometimes) satisfying self-indulgence of laying around and feeling sorry for yourself or thinking you can't create anything because your harasser has taken everything from you, and that may be something you want to choose for a while. But, when you are ready to move on from self-indulgence (and it might take a little while, I'm not saying there's anything wrong with indulging for however long you want), then it's time for the fun part of crushing your enemy with the beautiful life you create.

For some of my clients, choosing what they will create is natural and easy, but for many of them, objections come up about being broken or lost because of the trauma they have experienced (either in the form of the harassment itself or childhood abuse that has come up related to the harassment). Research shows that the most incredible creations and growth can come from trauma. This isn't an apology for trauma or an excuse to keep abuse alive so that we can all grow more. Unfortunately, we run into harassment and abuse whether we create something beautiful out of it or not.

Spiritual teachings often allude to the idea that it is through trauma that we grow and create, and that concept is supported by current scientific research. Probably every culture has a symbol for this idea: A diamond is made from tremendous pressure on coal; the white lotus grows from the muck; the phoenix rises from the ashes; pearls are made from sand irritating a clam; a broken and crushed seed sprouts with life.

While I would never wish trauma on anyone, each of us experiences it, and then we have a choice about whether to let it stop us or break us open and allow something beautiful to grow from us.

Post-Traumatic Growth

Many of my clients are diagnosed with PTSD before their legal case is resolved. Particularly, when my clients have tried to ignore harassing behavior for a long time, their bodies absorb the stress of trying to resist what's happening to them and trauma builds up. When we are first experiencing harassment, especially when we're at the top of our field in a professional setting, it can be shocking and it is typical to think, "There is no way this is really happening to me." When trauma builds up because we have not been able to process our experiences, it can create PTSD.

PTSD has a complicated set of disputed qualifications in the (the DSM, which mental health providers use to identify mental health disorders for insurance purposes). I am definitely not a psychiatrist, so take everything I say here with that in mind, but I have worked with dozens of people diagnosed with PTSD over the years and researched the topic in order to better help my clients. In my experience, PTSD becomes most extreme when my clients feel like they have no framework to process an experience they have. This either happens because the experience is so violent and overwhelming that they instinctively believe they might die (as with sexual assault) or because they try to ignore behavior for so many years that the resistance to processing it builds up.

Not everyone who experiences trauma develops PTSD. Researchers have done fascinating studies on why some people develop PTSD, and become stuck in the trauma experience, while others go on to experience some of the greatest growth of their lives. This research is so new that it's not very satisfying yet, and the recommendations tend to be: "have friends," "do fun things," "paint," "find other people like you," "maybe

Jesus?" I find those recommendations underwhelming because they are so specific and vague at the same time.

What the research seems to agree about, though, is that in order to move past trauma, it is important to "process" it. Let's just assume for the sake of argument that you've experienced some trauma, whether or not it's from sexual harassment. I'm assuming that you have had some trauma because in my view, everyone has experienced some trauma. The world is sharp.

"Processing" trauma, or any kind of negative experience or feeling, means integrating it into your larger memory of your life. MRI studies show that when we experience something particularly threatening to our life, the life-threatening memory can be stored in a different part of our brains than our normal life story. This is why flashbacks happen. A flashback happens when that segregated memory somehow gets triggered and it pops into our consciousness. The problem is that while normal memories might gently float to our consciousness like a dream, flashbacks are stored in our brains in such a way that they come back to us as though the event is literally happening to us again, right then and there. This is clearly a problem if you, like, ever want to go see a movie again and not be put back into your trauma experience.

The more a flashback comes to us, the more we are imprinting a path from our normal life back to the trauma experience. So, seemingly small events – like picking up a child's toy or a co-worker touching us on the shoulder – can throw us back into a life-threatening experience as though it is happening to us again in that moment. Bessel van der Kolk talks more about the science behind this in *The Body Keeps the Score*. I recommend looking into that book only if you want to nerd out on the options for PTSD treatment, and not if you are actually experiencing PTSD. It includes a lot of case studies that are very disturbing and triggering.

If you think you might have this type of segregated memory that jumps back into your life so that it feels like you are re-experiencing the trauma now, there are successful treatments for that, and I strongly encourage you to look into them. The evidence-based treatments that I have been most impressed by are EMDR (Eye Movement Desensitization and Reprocessing) and Somatic Experiencing.

Somatic Experiencing is the gentler of the two therapies and Peter Levine's book *Waking the Tiger* is a wonderful read if you are at all interested in exploring that therapy (that one is helpful to read even if you are experiencing PTSD now). Somatic Experiencing involves reframing your memories of what happened *around* the trauma – for example in the days leading up to it – to gently start reclaiming your power over your place in the traumatic memory.

EMDR is a lot more like magic, in the sense of "WTF, why does that work??" But, it has been shown to be successful, so I'm a big fan. (Note: not everyone is a fan of it, and I have heard opinions on both sides.) In EMDR, you have some kind of outside stimulus, like in some cases a therapist will have you hold a device in your right hand and one in your left and they will alternate vibrating between the two hands. In other cases, the therapist will hold something up to your face that forces you to look back and forth to the left and right.

As this happens, you go into the memory of your trauma. This has been shown to physically reprocess the segregated memory into your normal chronological memory of your life. So, basically, as the different sides of your brain are stimulated while you re-experience the memory, it allows your brain to reabsorb the memory, which it previously stored in a separate part of your brain, into the part of your brain with the normal stream of memory. This is similar to how your brain processes your memories during REM sleep.

The main lesson is this: You can't process a memory and grow from it if you are resisting that it is part of your life. That doesn't mean you have to think of yourself as a victim or believe you deserve bad things, but when you are resisting a memory (and your brain may be unconsciously doing that as part of a self-preservation mechanism), it puts you in a struggle with reality that leaves you powerless. You may be able to live a totally successful life without processing the memory and growing from it, but on some level, resisting the memory forces you to maintain a struggle with reality that sucks your energy away.

Like we talked about in Chapter 4 when we discussed doing the math instead of the drama, your brain is always working very hard to protect you from threats and to save energy. When your brain believes a memory is a threat, it is willing to put a tremendous amount of energy into separating that memory from the regular story of your life. In this situation, the memory itself becomes what your brain thinks is a giant tiger trying to attack you. If you can redirect your brain to allow the memory of trauma to reintegrate as part of the story of your life (not on your own, but with support), and you are not spending unconscious mental energy trying to resist the memory, then think of the energy you will have left over to create the life you want.

I am not saying you have to get therapy or process any memory. You don't have to do anything, and all of this is available as a support for you. If you do decide that you are ready to process a memory, make sure you have support systems around you that feel safe. But, what I am saying is that processing and accepting trauma experiences creates power over those experiences. It also exercises emotional and mental muscles that make you a stronger person and help you see how much strength you've shown in your life.

Most, if not all, of our life experience is memory. Right now, I have written these sentences, and each one is a developing memory. Ignoring trauma memories separates you from part of yourself and your life experience. Sometimes that feels like the only option, or at least the only safe option, and that is fair. When we are victimized as children, we truly are powerless against the adults around us. But, when we are separating ourselves from our childhood memories and rejecting those experiences, it keeps us in a powerless place over those memories. The more you separate from your memories and your experiences of life, the more you are cut off from yourself. These can become tiny deaths. The purpose of this is not to re-traumatize yourself by going back into traumatic memories, but to take back power, now as a safe adult, over the story of your life.

Think about someone who has been through an excruciatingly difficult, exhausting experience like the Olympics. Probably, Olympic athletes feel like their bodies aren't going to make it, and even have their bodies collapse in pain sometimes. This is so worth it to them because they know in the end they will be the best in their field and they will compete with other athletes at the top of their game. All of the pain, collapse, and exhaustion is worth it because of their goal. At any point, they could give up and decide not to experience the physical pain it takes to reach greatness.

That's how I think of trauma, and I don't mean to trivialize it at all or say trauma is something we should seek out and perpetuate. (On the other hand, I don't think physical collapse from exhaustion is a good thing or something I would seek out, either, but I do have tremendous respect for Olympic athletes who have most, if not all, probably experienced that.) The way I think of it is that each of us has trauma in our lives, and it is like an invitation from the Universe, saying, "Here is the training field for your particular greatness. What will you create with this trauma?" It is like your soul's obstacle course, challenging you to whatever your next level of growth could be.

Think of yourself, standing on an obstacle course, like you're on *American Gladiator* or *The Biggest Loser* or *Survivor*. Whatever show. You pick your show. You've got some kind of crazy jousting challenge, and another crazy monkey bars challenge, and another crazy challenge where you have to jump on pods over water. This obstacle course is bananas. And different versions of you are standing at each challenge. It's your job to create the story of that obstacle course and the woman who took it on.

A lot of times, our stories look like, "Don't talk about the monkey bars! That was painful!" or "I can't believe monkey bars happened to me! There must be something wrong with me that I had that obstacle" or even "I fell into the water on the pods challenge, so you can't expect me to face another challenge."

Olympic athletes don't just wake up one morning, go outside, and dominate an obstacle course. Honestly, I don't think they have obstacle courses in the Olympics, but you know what I mean. Olympic athletes have coaches and trainers and skilled support staff to get them to their highest goal. Olympic athletes get to their goal by embracing and envisioning each step of their success and incorporating all of that pain into the story of how they got there.

What I often see with clients is like the stories we could tell about our obstacle course. They avoid their trauma, blame themselves, and want to give up. This is normal, and please don't take anything I'm saying as more evidence that you are doing anything wrong. There is no way to do trauma wrong. But it misses out on using trauma for growth. An athlete grows if she falls into the water, climbs out, and starts again. An athlete grows if she learns from the past version of herself who felt pain on the monkey bars, not if she rejects that version of herself.

When we reject part of our lives, it becomes a small suicide that can later turn into a much larger rejection of life.

I hear you say that I don't know your trauma and I don't know what you've been through. That is true. But, I do know you are here to grow and you are capable of it. I know that about you without any doubt.

I'll say it again, life is sharp. If life cuts you, it is better to tend to the wound than pretend the blade doesn't exist or blame yourself for encountering it. In the same way, when we can accept that trauma exists, that our harassment happened, it becomes a starting point for what we can create out of it.

─────────── **ACTION STEPS** ───────────

Email me at Meredith@FreedomResourceCenter.com to get a copy of the Personal Career Defense Toolkit. Include "Toolkit" in the subject line of your email. Or, find your own notebook or blank sheet of paper to fill out these steps.

Make sure that wherever you write this, it includes a notice that what you write is in anticipation of talking with an attorney and pursuing a legal claim. That means it should be attorney-client or work-product privileged. Talk with an attorney in your state to get the details of what that means.

1. If nothing could hold you back, what would you create in your life?
2. What are you avoiding in your life?
3. What is that avoidance creating instead of what you want to create?

Chapter 9

——— 🌿 ———

Strategy 7: Purpose

Choosing your own purpose and going for it is the best form of resistance and revolution possible. You taking up space in the world for good and in line with your purpose, in and of itself, is a huge step toward defending your career from harassment and setting an example for other women who want to do the same. When you become small and get out of the way for harassment, you let harassment take up space. When you become big, and you set impossible, outrageous goals for what you want to create, harassment has to get smaller to get out of your way.

You can't talk about purpose without talking about Viktor Frankl, who used his time in the Nazi concentration camps Auschwitz and Dachau, to reach enlightenment. Don't worry. If you're not yet enlightened from the harassment you've experienced, there's still time. Among other earth shatteringly brilliant advice in *Man's Search for Meaning*, Frankl says, "Everything can be taken from a man but one thing: the last of the human freedoms – to choose one's attitude in any given set of circumstances, to choose one's own way."

Frankl says that choosing who we are, even in the most abusive circumstances (or particularly in abusive circumstances) is what creates

97

meaning, and meaning is more motivating and fulfilling than comfort or happiness. Frankl says, "What man actually needs is not a tensionless state but rather the striving and struggling for some goal worthy of him. What he needs is not the discharge of tension at any cost, but the call of a potential meaning waiting to be fulfilled by him." We are not fulfilled by ease, we are fulfilled by fighting toward impossible goals.

Women are often taught that our purpose is to get married and have children. Even if you were not directly taught this, like I was, you still have probably absorbed some of this message if you've ever seen a Disney movie. Or any movie ever. I was raised to believe that women had some kind of evil in them that required them to defer to the opinions of men, who were not cursed with the evil. So that was kind of intense, but not actually that different than a lot of the messages that are just assumed in TV, movies, and advertising in popular culture. Take the conversations about Hillary Clinton over the past few decades – no one is exactly sure what's wrong with her, but they're sure there is something wrong with her. It all assumes the lesson that it is wrong for women to have a public, visible, creative purpose beyond having children.

(Obligatory clarification that there's nothing wrong with being a mother or having children. *Obviously*.)

But, your children are not your purpose. Your children are wonderful, I'm sure, and wrangling them into the respectable humans they are today was an amazing feat that I have tremendous respect for. Still, they are not your purpose. I'll tell you why: because no matter how much time you've poured into them, no matter how much you've sacrificed for them or how amazing they are, it is too much pressure to put on another human to require them to be your purpose. Your children are supposed to mess up, and that is supposed to be out of your control. If you require your children to be your purpose, you become their victim when they can't follow through for you.

That's miserable. It makes you powerless over what your life is meant to create because you're relying on the judgment of a child, and it puts pressure on your child to pretend to live your life, not hers, just to maintain a relationship with you.

The other major trap I see people fall into is waiting for their purpose to announce itself. Like, we think we're going to walk into Starbucks one day, and Barack Obama is going to come up to us and be like, "You look like you were meant to be a famous foreign correspondent for CNN," and then we'll be like, "Whoa, Barack, I hadn't thought about it before, but you know, you're probably right. I do have a knack for packing travel shampoo without spillage." No, that is not how you find your purpose.

Luckily, it's easier than that.

Here's how you find your purpose. First, consider what makes you weird and awkward. What were you embarrassed about in high school? What did you try to hide to fit in?

For me, I am too opinionated and contrary. In high school, I pretended to have a smaller vocabulary than I actually had because my friends didn't understand the words I used. Boys didn't like me because I argued and pointed out the movies they liked were dumb. These are just a couple of examples of what I wanted to stifle in myself so that I could fit in. But, these were exactly the things that make me a great lawyer and coach.

I spent years fighting those parts of myself, and that fight early on manifested in suicidal thinking. I poured energy and time into struggling with and resisting suicidal thoughts. And, there are many ways that I see the women I work with choose small deaths – small suicides – no matter how hard they have worked or how successful they appear on the outside. Some of the most successful, and some of the most spiritual people I have worked with struggle with suicidal thinking, and it makes sense. It often starts with noble "self-sacrifice." We take the weird things about ourselves, the things that stand out and actually make us beautiful, and hide them so that other people can be comfortable. We start to think of the sacrifices we make as the value we are contributing to the people around us.

Not to ruin a classic for you, but this is what Shel Silverstein's *The Giving Tree* is about and why it is pretty problematic. Look at yourself as a giant oak tree in a forest of spindly pines. As you start growing, you realize that your gnarly, sprawling branches grow out toward your neighbors, while your pine tree neighbors take up as little space as possible and are basically sticks, stuck in the ground. You think, "There's something wrong with me, and I better not crowd my friends." You try to tuck your branches in on themselves, but it doesn't work, so all you're left with is cutting them off. This is like how we try to cut off the parts of ourselves that make us big and unique in order to make other people comfortable.

There is nothing wrong with trying to contribute positively to the lives of the people you care about, but that is very different than assuming your wild branches hurt other people. Cutting off what is wild and embarrassing about you is cutting off your purpose. It is its own form of suicide.

Especially when it comes to men, this can be very difficult because men are often raised to be too sensitive and fragile to know how to handle women being human. Men are often raised to think they deserve to have women obey them, and so when women do not, they can go so far as becoming violent, like Lundy Bancroft's man who thinks he owns the park. In order to choose life and purpose, it often requires us to let other people, including men, feel anger, grief, humiliation, shame, and other negative feelings of their own. Choosing life and purpose does not mean you have to bulldoze people or be a jerk, and it does not mean you have to put yourself in danger, it just means setting free those parts of yourself that you have resisted and tried to cut off. It means spreading out your branches. You can do this in small doses, and just test out your own thoughts and feelings about the reaction you get and then stop if things become too intense.

It means failing, failing again, and failing better, as Pema Chodron says. It does not mean being graceful the first time. When a baby takes control of her arms and legs to learn to walk, it is not graceful or pretty, but each fall strengthens her. Every time she crashes into something and faceplants and picks herself up again, no matter how many tears are involved, it is part of the inevitable process of her learning to walk. We have no doubt she will learn, and the painful process is worth it.

The same is true for capturing your purpose. When you decide to cultivate the weird, embarrassing, vulnerable part of you that bumps into your neighbors too much, it is not supposed to be pretty or easy, but it is *definitely* worth it.

When I am talking to my clients about choosing to be big in their purpose, they often object, "But, I don't want to be selfish!" They think that the alternative to being self-sacrificing is to be selfish. But, really, those two extremes are not the only options. In some ways, also, cutting off parts of yourself to avoid feeling embarrassment can be selfish. For example, my opinions, contrariness, and willingness to tell men when they're wrong has created incredible results for my clients. What if I decided to keep killing off those parts of myself just to avoid feeling embarrassment? That seems very selfish. At the same time, my willingness to contradict men in authority positions for my clients is not comfortable for the men in authority. It is so worth sacrificing my comfort and the comfort of men in authority to get my clients great results.

In order to follow your purpose, understand that you are agreeing to embrace failure and discomfort. Your failure and discomfort will inevitably create great things for the people who need you and they will probably create a ton of discomfort for people who want to keep you small. Do you want to be selfish for your people or for the people who want to keep you small?

If you are "avoiding" being selfish by silencing, limiting, or restricting yourself or cutting parts of yourself off, just understand that you are taking the side of your harasser. You have joined his team, instead of doing the hard work to become strong and big enough to serve the people who need you.

Most of us take the side of our harasser and are our own worst critics, at least at some point in our lives. It takes deliberate work to become your own advocate instead of your own prison guard.

Another way to capture your purpose is to think about it this way: Picture yourself as a disembodied soul, floating around before this life and hanging out with God or the Universe or whoever, before you decided to come to Earth. It doesn't matter what your spiritual beliefs are because it's just a thought exercise. And then you decided to choose this lifetime because you knew it would give you exactly the challenges you needed to grow into who you wanted to become. Why did you choose the exact harassment you are experiencing right now? Why do you have the qualities that stood out and were embarrassing in high school? What was this harassment meant to bring out in you and what are you meant to bring to other people through this experience?

Or, here's another way to look at it. There's a future version of you. She's solved all of the problems you have right now, and she's living the exact ideal life for you. She's looking back on what you're experiencing right now, and she thinks, "Wow, I never could have gotten here or become this strong if it weren't for those challenges." What was she meant to bring into the world because of the challenges you are facing now? In other words, why was it important for her to go through what is happening to you now? How is she uniquely qualified to share something important with the world?

I do not mean at all to trivialize your experience. My clients have experienced death threats, sexual assault, physical violence, kidnapping, stalking, and the daily humiliation of sexist ridicule, touching, and financial threats around being overlooked for promotion or losing their jobs for standing up for themselves. This is serious, sometimes life-threatening cruelty. I don't know your experience, but, in some ways, I may because I have experienced threats, kidnapping, stalking, and the humiliation of unwanted, repeated, back rubs, too. It may sound like I'm saying, "Don't worry about any of that and just show up as a free-spirited interpretive dancer!" That is far from what I'm saying. Unless somehow you are literally employed as an interpretive dancer, in which case, I support you in continuing to do your job.

What I am actually saying is that this is very, very serious. This is a crossroads in your decision about whether you will fight against yourself and be on the side of your harasser or if you will fight for your own life and take massive action to fulfill your purpose. It may seem like you can stay in a safe-zone of inaction, but really that is giving space to your harasser and choosing his side.

Developing your purpose and taking concrete steps towards strengthening it and building it is the best way to fight harassment.

Ninja Move

You have to be really clear on your purpose before taking these next steps, but since you've come this far with me, I think you're ready. Once you have chosen a purpose that is clear in your mind, and you are ready to go for it, no matter what kind of opposition you face, your brain starts to open up to see how even opposition can contribute to your purpose.

In *The Art of Learning*, Josh Waitzkin (the chess prodigy on whose life the movie *Searching for Bobby Fisher* was based) talks about learning how to be a "push hands master." Push hands is the Tai Chi fighting technique, and it is based on using other people's weight in order to knock them off balance. Waitzkin talks about learning to stand in a grounded position as though rooted, and he describes that this is the only way to maintain balance and use a competitor's force against him.

The same is true with purpose. When you have a purpose that resonates with your soul, it connects you to this life and this body, rather than keeping you in a place of struggle with yourself. The next question is, how can your harasser's force contribute to that purpose and that rooting?

This doesn't mean that you learn to love the harassment or appreciate it, although that is possible if you want it. This doesn't even necessarily mean that you learn to just let go of wanting the harassment to change when it won't. It means that you learn to actively use the force of the harassment in your favor.

So, for example, I worked with a woman whose supervisor thought she had called him out in public for being sexist, when she had no intention of doing that. He was so upset that he yelled at her, while sitting at a table full of colleagues, telling her that she was a liar and that he would not support her receiving a large commission she was due at the end of the year from the company. A couple of days later, having calmed down, he told her he wanted to apologize because he thought she might have taken his "joke" about her commission seriously.

Now, she could have struggled with his version of reality and tried to argue him into understanding that calling a threat a "joke" makes it worse, not better (and is also an insult to comedy). Instead, she accepted his apology and used it as part of her larger effort to disrupt the sexist nature of the company. She reported the incident, including his calling the threat a "joke." She accepted that he had his version of reality, rather than arguing with it, and used it as an example of the company trivializing threats and retaliation. She not only protected her own commission by doing that, but she was able to ask for more institutional forms of change regarding the pay for all women in the company.

I sometimes see this with very skilled, confident social media presences, where they will get a troll, and then use the troll to their own advantage. This is different than just ignoring the troll and understanding that you do not need to become smaller because of him. That in itself is a huge step that is worthy of congratulations. But, it is so much more fun to take the troll energy and use it in your favor.

Often, harassment involves "gaslighting" – or the harasser reinventing the history of a harassing incident. This is only a problem if we want the harasser to accept our version of reality and somehow think that matters. Usually, we get involved in this kind of mind-reading because we think that if we can understand what our harasser is thinking, it will keep us safe, but instead it takes us out of our integrity and purpose and into other people's minds. If you are focused on your purpose and how someone's problem behavior can contribute to it, you can find a way to make that happen, no matter what their version of reality is. Doing this lets you find work that is fulfilling and advance in it, no matter what anyone else is doing.

ACTION STEPS

Email me at Meredith@FreedomResourceCenter.com to get a copy of the Personal Career Defense Toolkit. Include "Toolkit" in the subject line of your email. Or, find your own notebook or blank sheet of paper to fill out these steps.

Make sure that wherever you write this, it includes a notice that what you write is in anticipation of talking with an attorney and pursuing a legal claim. That means it should be attorney-client or work-product privileged. Talk with an attorney in your state to get the details of what that means.

1. What personality traits made you awkward and embarrassed in high school? What purpose for your life can you find in those traits?

2. Why did past-you choose the exact struggles you are facing now? What did she know about how they are contributing to your purpose?

3. What would future you say about why you are facing harassment now? How will this contribute to becoming the ideal version of you?

4. Bonus: How can you use the energy of the harassment you are experiencing to contribute to your purpose?

Chapter 10

What Next?

"So, should I bring a case?" I hear you ask. As with all things in the law, the answer is "It depends." (Now you know the secret to why people love lawyers so much!) When someone comes to me and asks, "Do I have a case?" my initial thought is that the person has a pretty basic misunderstanding of what it means to use the law. You *always* have a case. I could sue you for taking breaks while reading this book. I would lose the lawsuit because it's not illegal for you to take breaks, but if I wanted to spend the money, I could still file a lawsuit over it. Then, you could sue me for filing a frivolous lawsuit, and we could spend all our days filing paperwork. Yay! If that's how we want to spend our time. So, yes, you have a case. Whether you should bring a case is another question.

The law is one way to set consequences for someone's harassing behavior, and sometimes it is a really important part of a career defense plan. Sometimes, it is a really, really effective way to set a consequence. It is reporting to the next level of authority (an agency or a court) and that authority has the power to hold your harasser accountable. Your harasser could go to jail or could have to pay money for what he did.

Unfortunately, there are a lot of reasons why things don't work out that way. You call the police, and they don't want to get involved because you don't have a restraining order. You talk to other lawyers, and they say that it will be difficult to prove what's happening to you because you don't have witnesses. Or, they say to call them back if you get seriously hurt or lose your job because of the harassment. These are really common problems with legal claims and often discourage women from advocating for themselves at all.

The reality is that the justice system is purposely set up so that it is very, very difficult to put someone in prison (unless it's a drug-related crime and they're black, but that's a whole different book). The law puts a lot of expectations on victims as to how they report, what they report, what they document, and how they present in court, in order to take away someone's freedom. I don't necessarily disagree with this in theory, but it is a system set up to protect men from the power of the government, not set up to protect women from men. So, when you are using the justice system, whether criminal or civil, you need to be very strategic in the way you use it.

What I see is that all too often this is prohibitively overwhelming for my clients, even if they have support. When I see women trying to navigate this system alone, I am never surprised to see them give up. There are supposed to be support systems in place like a victim services office in the district attorney's office or a sexual assault support agency or a women's shelter. But, these services are so overworked and understaffed that they rarely have time to put attention to your individual issue.

Then, when you hire your own attorney, that attorney has been trained to diagnose whether your situation falls into a very specific set of parameters set by the law to determine if you get money. The attorney may say, "Well, there's no insurance," so it is not worth bringing a claim. Or, the attorney may say, "The law doesn't apply to this situation, unfortunately." And those could be pieces of important legal advice.

But, it does not mean that is the end of your experience or your experience just goes away. There is always something you can do to defend your career, and to move forward to use your experience as a platform for the next step of your life. I'm not being optimistic in saying that. It is grueling work. And you are up to it. It is your work to do. Whether or not you have a legal claim, whether or not you want to bring a legal claim, it is your work to do.

With help.

Should you bring a legal claim? Yes, if that is the next step to set consequences and leverage your purpose in life to take you to the next level of who you were meant to be. If it is the best way to defend your career, yes, you should file a legal claim. You will be a hero for your community, even if they don't appreciate it.

Or, no. If filing a legal claim is torture and a way to keep you involved in the harassment you've experienced, then, no, you should not file a legal claim. If it will entangle you in years of expenses and drama and stress, if it will keep you involved in seeing your harasser and tied to him, then, no, you should not file a legal claim.

The trick is that in almost every legal claim, both experiences can be true. If you are happy with your reason for filing a legal claim, then you are in the best position possible to make a good decision.

When I first became a lawyer, I was very, very unhappy. I loved my clients, don't get me wrong, but they had been through horrific experiences, and I was not sure I was actually helping them. I would write letters and complaints describing that their lives were over because of their trauma, and if they were lucky, they would get money. Our office would give them the money and basically say, "Congratulations! Your life is still over, but here's some money!"

That did not sit right with me for a number of reasons. First, I did not really believe my clients' lives were over, no matter what trauma they experienced. I knew my clients were resilient, but I didn't know how to help them access that resilience and recover. I knew I wasn't their therapist and I didn't want to be their therapist. I didn't know it then, but I wanted to help them take their trauma experience and create the exact life they wanted in spite of it (or even because of it). I loved watching the strength and courage my clients had in standing up for themselves, but I didn't want my only contribution to their lives to be getting them a little bit of money (if they were lucky). In bringing a civil legal claim, all there is to work with is money, but every amount of money seems small and trite compared to the gravity of a trauma experience. My clients were great warriors, and I felt like I was throwing some dollar bills at them for their trouble.

Recovering money for my clients is an important part of my job, but it is not always possible, even with deserving clients, and it was not enough.

I developed the strategies I describe in this book because I want to contribute to my clients' growth through their experience of harassment and trauma. I want my clients to actually end harassment in their lives for good and move on to greater battles and putting their energy into creating what they were meant to create. I want them to defend their careers from harassment and thrive in fulfilling work. I have seen my clients come out on the other side of a legal claim completely transformed from victim to warrior. That is what I want to see for you.

You may already know you are a warrior and only want support with a few details of how the law applies to your situation. That is okay too! I imagine if you have come this far in this book that you want more for your life and your career than a lawsuit, but many attorneys only handle the legal side, and that is the right path for some people.

The real reason to talk with me or another lawyer is to take control over your circumstances and make sure they are serving you and your career. Traditional law will diagnose whether you can bring a claim for money in court, and there are thousands of good attorneys around the country who can help you figure that out. That is not enough for me. I can help you with that, but I also want to help you strategize how to take the most power and control over your life and create exactly what you want.

I want to see you take the ultimate step of resistance and grow to the next level of who you can become.

I was talking with a colleague about a client who had attempted suicide after a sexual assault. In that year, I worked with the highest number of clients so far who let me know they had actually made suicide attempts, and I also had the highest number of people tell me that our conversations helped them resolve suicidal thinking and move forward. Intense! I was talking with my colleague to find out what she thought about how my client's suicide attempt might affect her legal case. Unfortunately, it was something the jury would probably need to hear about in my client's case. My colleague said, "Well, who hasn't thought about killing herself?"

That comment really struck me because I had to agree that it has become incredibly normal, especially for women, to practice self-harm, give in to defeat, and even attempt suicide. No wonder, too. Everything outside of us in culture tells us that if we work hard enough, we can have whatever we want. So, when we face confusing messages that demean us for trying to have what we want and being women at the same time (and even worse if you are a woman of color), it is easy to think that we just don't belong and there is something wrong with us. "Why is this happening to me?" we ask, as though there is something we've done to create the sexism in our lives.

That is the vulnerable place that many of my clients are in when they come to me for career defense training. They have tried ignoring harassment, have quit jobs and relationships to get away from it, and most of them have even tried some form of counseling therapy. But, they still find themselves wondering if the harassment is their fault and worrying that their trauma means something is wrong with them. Despite what they have tried, they are often telling their story in a way that blames themselves for other people's harassing behavior.

Whether my clients decide to make legal claims or not, in my career defense trainings, I work with them to practice the skills to end harassment for good. I often see my clients go from being their own worst harassers to strong self-advocates. Seeing them develop actionable plans for ending harassment in their lives and creating what they were meant to create is more valuable than any money I can recover for them.

—————————— ACTION STEPS ——————————

Are you wondering if you have a legal claim? What is waiting to take action costing you? I developed a confidential assessment checklist that you can download and go over in the privacy of your own home to help you understand if your career is safe from sexism. You can get the assessment at

https://freedomresourcecenter.com/is-your-career-safe

If you have questions for me about how the law and these self-advocacy principles apply to your case, send me an email at meredith@ freedomresourcecenter.com

Conclusion

If you have worked hard to get to where you are in your career, but you're worried you're going to have to give up everything you've worked for because of harassment, talk to me. I hope this book has given you an overview of what is possible in your life and how you can use your experience of harassment as a starting point to become the powerful presence you were meant to be.

I want to see you take up space. Take up all the space you've been given, and then grow to take up more. I want to see you be the most powerful person, the biggest energy, in every room you enter. When I take my clients through a legal case, I want to know they can get on the stand and command the attention of the entire jury and judge with their story. And each of them gets there.

They don't start out that way. I didn't start out that way. Taking power over your life is hard work, and it requires you to lean into the sharpness of life. My clients learn how to be curious about the harassment they are experiencing, but to ask themselves the right questions about it.

My clients come to me asking, "What did I do to deserve this?" and they leave asking better questions like, "How is this going to help me?" They don't make that transition because of wishful, forced, positive thinking. They make that transition out of commitment to what they are meant to create in the world, courage to be vulnerable and fail, and a willingness to do the hard work of getting up again every time they fall down.

They commit to breaking the cycle of making themselves small and giving up space to avoid harassment.

Too often I talk to women who leave job after job, career after career, to avoid harassment. This ends up costing them probably hundreds of thousands of dollars and years of their life, trying to avoid harassment. It seems like the easy solution at the time and sounds easier than confronting harassment and dealing with it, but really, ignoring and avoiding harassment is much, much more work and incredibly expensive. Traditional law firms try to do what they can to help women with legal claims, but they are limited in truly ending harassment in their clients' lives. Often women resolve one claim, but then go on to continue to experience harassment in another job or career.

Here is a recap of the strategies I will teach you if we work together to develop a personalized career defense plan:

Strategy 1: Law. Many women come to me having tolerated harassment in misery for years, not really understanding whether the law applied to them. Using this strategy, I get a clear picture of the current situation, walk you through how the law applies to your situation, and help you understand what you need to do if you want to preserve or bring a legal claim. If you are in a state where I am not licensed to practice law, I use my network to find an attorney in that state who can advise you about the law in that state. We work together to figure out how to use the law in your favor.

Strategy 2: Reality. For many of my clients, it is one thing to understand what the law expects from them, but they fall into feeling overwhelm and even depression and despair when it comes to following through on what they need to do to apply it. Using this strategy, I get a clear understanding of the reality of your life, the obstacles you are facing, and the practical side of how to apply the law to your situation and get the most successful result. I use my personal and professional experience, as well as your unique understanding of the people involved, to decide the best course of action forward.

Strategy 3: Mapping. One of the biggest pitfalls I see for women who choose not to work with me is that they think changing their jobs or even leaving cities or careers will be enough to end harassment. That is almost never enough to really end harassment for good, and it ends up costing them time and money. Using the tools in the Mapping strategy, I teach you how to become stronger, more committed, more courageous, super-hero versions of yourself and end harassment for good in your life. We create a plan together for exactly what to do going forward and for what you need to think, how you need to feel, and what you need to do in order to get to your plan for success.

Strategy 4: Action. Many women do not even realize the small (or big) ways they are giving in to harassment by saying "yes" to make other people happy. Using the Action strategy, my clients learn to honor what they say "yes" to and be very deliberate about it. This strategy helps you become uncompromising about being your own advocate and on your own side.

Strategy 5: Consequences. When women leave careers because of harassment or in any way make themselves small, it actually rewards the harasser. It gives him no reason to change. Harassment gets bigger, and the next time you face harassment, it is even more difficult to shut it down. Using the Consequences strategy, I help you understand how to set clear boundaries, recognize boundary violations, and set consequences for them.

Strategy 6: Creation. Another huge pitfall I see many women fall into is that they start to get stuck in believing that harassment happens to them because there is something wrong with them or that they are broken. Your harassment may have involved trauma, but the research shows that it is possible to turn trauma into a place of amazing growth in your life. Using the Creation strategy, I help you develop a specific plan for what you want to create from your harassment experience.

Strategy 7: Purpose. When we think that life happens to us, instead of for us, we sit around and wait for our purpose to be revealed and we end up getting pushed from one harassing experience to another. In the worst-case scenario, when we give up this much power, we turn against ourselves and end up as our own worst harassers. Using the tools in the Purpose strategy, you are able to take power over your purpose in life and use it in your favor.

I apply each of these strategies in my career defense training so that my clients learn the skills to end harassment in their lives for good. This doesn't mean that they have sheltered themselves from any rude or inappropriate men and have to live isolated and alone. It means that when they encounter rude and inappropriate men, my clients understand so thoroughly how to set consequences and use the situation in their own favor that the harassment loses all of its power over them.

Look at it this way: If an eight-year-old boy did what your harasser is doing right now, would you leave your career because of it? Would you know what to do? Would you even call it harassment? Probably, you would understand that the child needed discipline, rather than obedience. You would feel confident in your ability to walk away or respond (whichever was best for you). You certainly would not spend time and money trying to hide from him or adjust yourself to his behavior.

You say that your situation is different and more threatening – your harasser actually has power over your finances or physical safety – and I hear you. I do not take your situation lightly. My dream for you is that you become the woman who is so strong, powerful, and courageous that she looks at what you are experiencing now and it seems like that eight-year-old boy to her. She is so in touch with her own power that she is to your harasser as you are now to the harassing child. Using the seven strategies to ending harassment, you can meet that future version of yourself and at least consider what she has to say.

The biggest trap I see women fall into is thinking they can put off dealing with harassment for just a few more months or a few more years. In terms of legal claims, they often pass their time limits and lose their right to sue because they think they can just put things off a little longer. In terms of their reality, the harassment they encounter gets worse and worse until they are willing to deal with it.

Many women believe they should just be able to handle a toxic work environment on their own. But, there's a reason you may not be able to do that: You were never taught. We all need outside support when we're learning a new skill. Take your career, and the women coming after you, seriously enough to get the help this situation deserves.

If you think you might be experiencing harassment or sexism, but you are not sure, you can download the free, confidential assessment at https://freedomresourcecenter.com/is-your-career-safe. Don't wait until you have lost your right to sue or until the harassment gets worse. It's time to take your power back.

Appendix I

---⚜---

Cease & Desist Sample

This is a sample of the letter I send out in appropriate cases for my clients. When I send this letter out, I make it clear that the harasser may not contact my client and must make all communication through me. In some situations, like when the harasser is your boss, you may have to have continued direct contact. This letter may be appropriate when it is possible for you to have no contact with your harasser, but only if you intend on never contacting the harasser again.

As always, this is meant to help you understand your options, but it is important to talk with an attorney about how the law applies to your individual case.

The Goddess Athena

123 Olympic Blvd.

Mount Olympus, Greece 10000

[DATE]

Via USPS and Personal Service

Pathetic Harasser

456 Lame Street

Washington, DC 20500

Re: CEASE AND DESIST NOTICE

Dear Pathetic Harasser:

I have previously notified you that all further contact is unwelcome on [DATE] by [MEANS (phone, text, email, etc.)]. Do not contact me or my family again, either directly or through third parties, about this letter or any other matter through any means of communication, including email, phone, text, social media, or in-person communications. All future communication from you to me or my family will be considered unwanted contact.

You are hereby directed to CEASE AND DESIST ALL CONTACT WITH ME OR MY FAMILY.

I am a respected professional. I have spent years serving the community and building a positive reputation as [PROFESSION]. Your violent and threatening behavior has interfered with my ability to continue with my work and feel safe in my home and in this community.

Specifically, the following behavior has made me reasonably fear for my safety and are examples of unwanted contact:

In [DATE], [CONTACT].

In [DATE], [CONTACT].

[MORE EXAMPLES]

I estimate that to date you have cost me and my family over $[ACCURATE ESTIMATE] in wage loss, property damage, and medical expenses alone. Some of the property you destroyed were priceless heirlooms that are irreplaceable. That amount does not even come close to the emotional damage for which you are responsible.

If you do not comply with this demand, you will expose yourself to a court order prohibiting you from contacting me and criminal charges. If you continue harassing, stalking, and menacing me, I plan to pursue all available legal remedies, including seeking money damages, protective order from the court, and an order that you pay my court costs and attorney fees. Your liability for such a lawsuit could be considerable.

I encourage you to talk with an attorney regarding this matter.

Sincerely,

[YOUR NAME]

cc: Any probation office, parent, or other person with authority over the harasser

Appendix II

——— ✲ ———

Report of Harassment Sample

Here is a sample email for reporting harassment to a supervisor or someone else who is able to step in and set a consequence for your harasser:

To: [Appropriate Reporting Person Email]

From: [Your Email]

Date:

Subject Line: Sexist Behavior

Hi [Reporting Person],

Thanks for talking today about [HARASSER]'s concerning behavior. I wanted to make sure what I told you today was clear, and so I thought I would follow up with this email. [HARASSER] has been [FILL IN SPECIFIC BEHAVIOR]. It is clear that he is doing this because I am a woman. The reason I can tell he is doing this because I am a woman is [REASON].

I love my job, and I want to be able to keep working here, but [HARASSER]'s behavior is interfering with my ability to do my job and I am starting to feel unsafe. I am worried he is going to continue [BEHAVIOR], which will interfere with my ability to do my job and make work feel threatening.

I want to do whatever I can to help work this out, but I can't work in an unsafe environment. Please let me know as soon as possible what the plan is to make this stop.

Thanks for your work on this.

[YOUR NAME]

Ninja Move:

Here is a sample email that you can use if you want to address the harassment directly with your harasser and try to get things to change that way:

To: [Harasser]

From: [Your Email]

Date:

Subject Line: Sexist Behavior

Hi [Harasser],

Thanks for talking today about your behavior. I wanted to make sure what I told you today was clear, and so I thought I would follow up with this email. You have been [FILL IN SPECIFIC BEHAVIOR]. It is clear that you are doing this because I am a woman. The reason I can tell you are doing this because I am a woman is [REASON].

I love my job, and I want to be able to keep working here, but your behavior is interfering with my ability to do my job and I am starting to feel unsafe. I understand, based on our conversation today, that you are willing to stop.

I want to do whatever I can to help work this out, but I can't work in an unsafe environment.

Thanks for agreeing to stop [BEHAVIOR].

[YOUR NAME]

Further Reading

The Gift of Fear by Gavin de Becker
Why Does He Do That? by Lundy Bancroft
Self Coaching 101 by Brooke Castillo
Awakening Compassion by Pema Chodron (Audio)
Man's Search for Meaning by Viktor E. Frankl
Essentialism by Greg McKeown
Grit by Angela Duckworth
The Dance of Anger by Harriet Lerner
The Life Changing Magic of Tidying Up by Marie Kondo
Backlash by Susan Faludi
Half the Sky by Nicholas D. Kristof and Sheryl WuDunn

Acknowledgments

This book could not have been written if it were not for Brooke Castillo, who said into my earbuds through her podcast a few years ago, "Your thoughts create your feelings." That sentence profoundly shifted my life and set me free.

This book would not have been written if it were not for Kathleen Karlyn, a film professor at the University of Oregon, who was the first person who said to me (or the first person I heard say, at least), "Feminism isn't about hating men, it's about helping women."

To the Honorable Suzanne Chanti, who said all you need to have in life is an open and fearless heart. She said there is no shame in falling down, but it's getting stuck there – that's the shame. Thank you for giving me the privilege of your company.

To the Honorable Ilisa Rooke-Ley, my mother-daughter-sister-friend, who has always expected the best for me and seen the best in me.

To Eliel Fionn, who told me my soul has majored in ending oppression. Time to use my major.

To the women who have bravely shared their stories with me and transformed their lives under my eyes. To all the women who were brave enough to post #MeToo and protest when a harasser took over our country, and to all the women too scared to speak out.

To my brother, who is smarter than me and has always listened to me anyway.

To Erica, Tracey, Sarah, Mandy, Erin, Linda, Amanda, Katie Laine, Lorelai, Levi, Cam, John, Bea, Tiffany, McKenzie, and all of the other dear friends who have fed me, gotten me drunk, and stood by me through the challenges that taught me what I needed to know to write this book.

To Angela Lauria, who I knew would be the perfect person courageous enough to yell at me into writing this book. Thank you to Mandy Vickers, Kim Benjamin, Caryn Gillen, Kara Loewentheil, Torie Henderson, Kim Taylor, Stacey Smith, Dan Smith, and the other coaches who have paved this path for me and helped me manage my mind.

To the Morgan James Publishing team: Special thanks to David Hancock, CEO & Founder for believing in me and my message. To my Author Relations Manager, Gayle West, thanks for making the process seamless and easy. Many more thanks to everyone else, but especially Jim Howard, Bethany Marshall, and Nickcole Watkins.

To my parents, without whom I would not have learned any of these lessons.

To the men who have stopped harassing me when I asked them to stop and shown embarrassment in their inappropriate behavior and courage in their willingness to change.

About the Author

Meredith Holley is a trial lawyer and life coach who helps successful, professional women overcome sexual harassment. After clerking for trial judges, Meredith joined a prestigious litigation firm as an advocate for employees who experienced discrimination. Meredith quickly realized that in order to truly overcome harassment and discrimination, her clients needed more than the law could offer.

Meredith became certified as a life coach through *The Life Coach School*, a boutique cognitive coaching school, and revolutionized her practice. Now, Meredith combines legal strategy, practical understanding of her clients' lives, and evidence-based cognitive management techniques. She develops individualized plans for her clients to overcome sexual harassment and thrive in their careers. Through her one-on-one programs, she works with her clients to execute those plans. Her clients have included other lawyers, professors, and women working in finance and construction.

Meredith is an Oregonian through and through, and she attended undergrad and law school at the University of Oregon. Raised in a strict religious home, and taught as a child that women were inherently evil, Meredith did not become a feminist until college. Since then, she has become a strong advocate for reconciliation between the genders.

As a Peace Corps volunteer in Ukraine, she developed a mentorship program between her high school students and girls in the local orphanage. Now, she works with Lane County Women Lawyers, the Trauma Healing Project, Oregon Trial Lawyers Association, and Trial Lawyers Care to advocate for gender equality, economic justice, and community building. She is a Reiki Master.

Meredith loves peonies, British zombies, and meditation. She looks back on each instance of harassment or discrimination she experienced (every unwanted back rub, every threat about her salary, every cat call, etc.) with gratitude for what it has taught her about ending those experiences for other people. She believes every woman deserves a thriving career, safe from sexual harassment.

Website: http://freedomresourcecenter.com

Email: Meredith@freedomresourcecenter.com

Facebook: https://www.facebook.com/freedomresourcecenter/

Thank You

When my clients first come to me, each of them has a unique story, but all of them have common themes. The shock, stress, and loneliness of trying to ignore and push through what is happening to them comes first. Then, the fear that something really is wrong with their experience. Then, ultimately the decision that they need to find out if there is something they can do about it.

My clients start out feeling isolated by their experience, but as the #MeToo and #TimesUp movements have shown, we are all connected by these experiences. Whatever yours is, you are not alone. I designed the free, confidential assessment "Is Your Workplace Safe From Sexual Harassment?" to help women understand if they are tolerating sexist behavior when they don't need to. It is available here: https://freedomresourcecenter.com/is-your-career-safe.

If you've taken the assessment and have questions about it or want to share your results, send me an email at Meredith@FreedomResourceCenter.com. I would love to hear about what you are doing to defend your career from harassment and to thrive in fulfilling work!

To get a copy of the Personal Career Defense Toolkit, where you can complete the activities listed in this book, email me at Meredith@FreedomResourceCenter.com, with "Toolkit" in the subject line, and I will send it over.